101 IDEAS

for Piano Group Class

Building an Inclusive Music Community for Students of All Ages and Abilities

By Dr. Mary Ann Froehlich

Editor: Judi Gowe Bagnato
Cover Art and Illustrations: Rama Hughes
Book Layout: Nancy Rehm

© 2004 Summy-Birchard Music division of Summy-Birchard Inc. exclusively distributed by
Alfred Music Publishing Co., Inc.
All Rights Reserved.   Printed in USA.

ISBN-10: 1-58951-402-5
ISBN-13: 978-1-58951-402-7

Dedicated to –

My parents, who made countless sacrifices to provide me with an exceptional music education. My extraordinary piano teachers, who gave me the gift of music which changed my life. My children, Janelle, Natalie, and CJ, and students, who have been expert instructors in piano pedagogy.

Acknowledgements

With many thanks to –

Judi Gowe Bagnato and my friends at Warner Bros., who caught the vision of this project and made it a reality.

My husband, John, for his constant love, support, and generosity in sharing his computer expertise.

The contributors who graciously shared their stories in Chapter 12 and continue to inspire me with their lives.

TABLE OF CONTENTS

Introduction

I never intended to become a private piano teacher. Did you? If you are like me, you experienced many unexpected twists and turns in your life that led to your current vocation.

Trained as a performer and a music therapist, I was passionate about using music and other creative arts to help children in pain. Along the journey, I studied the Suzuki Method as part of my graduate training. I found it interesting but not relevant to my work in a children's hospital with chronically and terminally ill patients. I mentally filed it away.

But then when I became a new mother I remembered the Suzuki Method. I also remembered those piano pedagogy and music education courses. I chose to stay home with my daughter and wanted to teach her the joy of making music. I then began teaching other people's children in our home, and soon I was teaching children with special needs. I had come full circle. This adventure resulted in a book I wrote ten years ago for parents about music education in the home.

The book you are holding is not for parents. This book is a baton that I am handing to teachers. After parenting three children and planning classes for almost twenty years, I found group classes to be the core of my piano program. I hope to save you hours of groundwork and inspire you to use these ideas as a springboard for your own creative planning. Because I am a Suzuki piano teacher, you will find this program based on the Suzuki philosophy, but the ideas are applicable to any piano program. Once you begin the brainstorming process, your own ideas will flow and explode.

This is not a research book but is intended to be practical. It is designed as an interactive book, with questions that allow you to reflect on your own experience, and room to make notes and brainstorm about planning your group classes. Inserted between the chapters, you will find mental energizers, unusual insights into composers' family relationships, and information about composers' lives as students and teachers. These inserts will provide mental breaks between the material. I hope that this book will be a brain compatible experience for you.

The intent of this volume is to offer supplementary material and is no substitute for learning and polishing serious piano literature, the core experience of any piano program. This book should not be misunderstood as a group program with multiple keyboards. The one-on-one private lesson is the most effective way to teach students, and the group class is the celebration of shared learning. Nor is this a theory program. For those needs, I recommend Michiko Yurko's excellent books and games, such as Music Mind Games, which are assets to any piano program and can be incorporated into group class activities.

101 Ideas for Piano Group Class is divided into three sections. Part I lays the foundation for an educational philosophy. Part II focuses on ideas for piano group class. Part III discusses inclusion in practice and teaching piano students with special needs. Part II offers you practical, fun tools for planning your curriculum, while Part III encourages you to expand your music community with students of all ages and abilities. The two objectives are intertwined. Every student has unique needs and can thrive in a safe, nurturing music community.

When I was in graduate school, my music history professor would begin his Baroque music class by giving us problem-solving puzzles that had absolutely nothing to do with music. Finally we asked him why he tortured us with these mind games, and he answered as follows: "The most important thing I can teach you is to think outside the box, to see problems in a new way, and creatively solve them. Never approach a task in the same way just because that's how you've always done it. THINK. My hope is that you will become innovative teachers and creative problem solvers."

I also invite you to think outside the box – to think in new, creative ways about traditional challenges. I invite you to take your students on the adventure of creating a music community to celebrate the joy of music making.

Did you know?

Schoenberg

Schoenberg was a self-taught musician with little formal training. He was worshipped by his students, which included Berg and Webern. Schoenberg was a demanding teacher but developed close relationships with his students that lasted a lifetime. He wanted his students to use their own imaginations and not to copy rote exercises. Schoenberg believed that students were best educated through creative activity.

Stravinsky

Stravinsky was compulsive about his tidy work habits. He said, "The piano itself is the center of my musical discoveries." Though he struggled with the public's misunderstanding of his works, which included riots at some of his premieres, he ironically found Schoenberg's compositions to be unintelligible to him.

Chapter 1

> *Without the social and emotional context, there is no learning that can take place. The child has to feel safe. And if children do not feel safe, they can't absorb the cognitive lessons.*
>
> —Mona Hajjar Halaby

Cooperation—not competition—is one of the key principles of the Suzuki Method. Also, group classes are as important as individual private lessons. Violin group classes are well established, but it is a little more challenging to develop piano group classes.

The piano is different from any other instrument during the learning phase. While instrumentalists can play in bands and orchestras and vocalists can sing in choirs, pianists do not generally practice in groups. Practicing alone can be an isolating experience, which fits very few personalities.

Nevertheless, I contend that the "plight of the solo pianist" is a self-perpetuating myth. My daughter's violin teacher shared with me that her own daughter wanted to study the piano instead of the violin and wondered, "But what can she possibly do with that skill?" The teacher had played in orchestras throughout her life and saw piano study as a waste of time. Her view is all too common.

Relevancy is the key to education and inspiring students. Students want to learn a new skill when they see that it is relevant and useful in daily life. Learning must have a clear purpose and immediate application.

As we pianists know, playing the piano can be a relevant and social experience. We accompany choirs, vocalists, and instrumentalists. We play in ensembles, pit orchestras, and jazz bands. We accompany talent shows and sing-alongs. Countless musicians are always looking for a good accompanist. The opportunities are limitless.

Yet the piano is a difficult instrument to master. Pianists do not enjoy many social benefits (not to mention the extra money – something very relevant for young people) until they have advanced skills. How do we bridge the gap? How do we make music making relevant for beginning and intermediate pianists? The answer is to bring the group experience to students that is tailored to their level.

A regular piano group class offers students the opportunity to share with one another and enjoy making music as a group. Competition of any kind is inappropriate. Learning together – cooperation – is the goal. Webster's dictionary defines cooperation as association with others for mutual benefit. Even more important than cooperation is celebration. The goal is to develop a passion for music making in our students.

Music educators and music therapists usually have a solid background in educational theory. As music majors, pianists are seldom required to take education classes. Beyond piano pedagogy classes (which too often focus on technical skills and methods), piano teachers are often unfamiliar with the theory of how children and adults effectively learn, the principles of cooperative learning, brain-compatibility theory, and other critical information.

We commit a great disservice to the Suzuki tradition when we focus on Suzuki Method books and recordings without fully understanding his teaching philosophy. The Suzuki Method is applicable to any field of study. Suzuki was one of the most innovative educators of the past century, instinctively incorporating the most current learning principles, including the group process. Suzuki's goal was to develop "beautiful hearts" in children. Did you know that Suzuki often asked his students at the end of their lessons to report an act of kindness that they had performed during the week? That is "performance" with heart. For Suzuki, developing positive character traits was as important as developing musical skills.

The goal is thus to build a thriving music community that nurtures caring connections between its members.

What Is Cooperative Learning?

Sometimes the greatest gifts in life fall into our laps without our initial recognition. I was introduced to cooperative learning through two of my daughters' elementary school teachers over a four-year period. As a classroom volunteer, I began to observe real expertise in cooperative learning, and I was amazed at the results. Because cooperative learning is inclusive, these teachers encouraged me to partner with them in developing music and writer's workshop programs. They shared current research literature with me and even invited me to attend professional seminars with them. This opportunity changed not only my children's lives but mine as well.

Realizing that Suzuki viewed the group class as an important part of private instruction, I began to research how cooperative learning principles could be applied to piano study. It is important to understand that there are numerous cooperative learning methods and a variety of strategies, but the core principles remain constant in each approach. This is not a set curriculum but a dynamic process. The following is a summary of ten basic principles applied to music study.

Ten Principles of Cooperative Learning

1. Learning occurs naturally in small groups. The goals of music instruction, healthy social skills, communication, and the total well-being of each student can be met simultaneously. Teachers use a variety of strategies to accomplish these goals.

2. Competition is the opposite of cooperation and has no place in the group experience. Competition isolates, while cooperation creates community. We should never compare our children nor should we compare our students. A stressful environment where students feel judged is detrimental to their growth. Life should not be presented as a contest with winners and losers. Have you seen the motto: "Second place is just first loser"? Cooperation breeds creativity, but competition discourages risk taking. We must risk to create.

3. Small groups are safe places to learn, where participants build trust between each other and the leader. We are most receptive to learning when we feel safe, rather than stressed or threatened. Sharing our music with people who genuinely care about us is very different than performing for strangers. Cooperation is a learned skill that requires practice. It is one of the most important skills needed as adults in our work places and communities. Cooperative learning fosters resiliency. (See Chapter 11.)

4. Children's retention increases when they participate in interactive group learning. Cooperation involves working together towards a common goal. Each student can make a unique contribution. *Jigsawing* refers to a process where each student masters a separate "piece" and shares it with the group. If there are six members in a group, students gain six times as much information and experience as they would alone. Learning is multiplied in a group.

5. Students' families are extensions of the small group, which creates a safe environment. Parents and siblings are encouraged to participate in the piano group experience. Our goal is to build an inclusive music community.

6. The community circle, as practiced in the Tribes cooperative learning method, is similar to the music circle used by music therapists and Orff Schulwerk specialists. In this method, children are seated in a circle and encouraged to each share musically and personally with the full attention and respect of other students. No one is forced to share; each student has a right to pass.

7. Group processing, a time for students to reflect on how the group is working together, is part of the community circle experience. Brainstorming and problem-solving as a team are equally important.

8. Cooperative learning is student-centered, rather than teacher-centered. The teacher is no longer "the sage on the stage" but the "guide on the side." Teachers are not lecturers but mentors and facilitators of interactive learning experiences.

9. Energizers, fun activities designed to engage students, serve two group purposes: first, they encourage students in getting to know each other and give them a sense of belonging. Second, they energize children, literally waking them up and re-engaging them when they become bored and start to mentally drift from the group. Ice-breakers, silly games, and physical activities are all energizers. Sometimes called "brain recesses," these are excellent class openers and life savers halfway through class when students become inattentive. Music activities are natural energizers.

10. Inclusion is the key to a thriving community. No one is too old or too young to participate. Differences in abilities and learning styles are welcomed. Each student, regardless of age or ability, can make a contribution to group class and other students will benefit.

Drs. Roger and David Johnson are experts in this field and define five elements essential to all cooperative learning groups:

1. Positive interdependence (cooperation vs. competition)

2. Face-to-face interaction (students learning together)

3. Interpersonal social skills (students developing trust, respect, and healthy interactive skills)

4. Individual accountability (with each student responsible for learning and contributing to the group)

5. Group processing (students reflecting upon group effectiveness and ways to improve the process)

Jeanne Gibbs developed the Tribes cooperative learning method and she combines these five elements into three stages:

1. Inclusion – Students get to know one another.

2. Influence – Students value each other, their differences and contributions.

3. Community – Students work creatively together and celebrate learning.

As music teachers, we can see that cooperative learning researchers may use different terms to describe their methods, but the foundation does not change. More important, **music making is the most natural setting to encourage and celebrate cooperative learning.**

> *Ensembles are not just classes or performance groups, but guardians of their own specific culture, a culture that informs and enriches the lives of their members.*
>
> —Steven Morrison

Parent Support Groups

An added bonus in creating a music community of students and families is watching a parent support network develop. In some large piano programs, a parent support group can be a formal organization, complete with officers, fund raisers, frequent concerts, and a host of activities that support and compliment the teacher's work. I, however, personally prefer a natural parent support network, in which the focus remains on relationships. I recently heard about one Suzuki program that encourages the mothers of students to sometimes meet without their children. During their "moms night out," they become better acquainted and discuss how they help their children practice and share other tips. A buddy system can easily be formed, whereby veteran music moms encourage mothers of beginners and are available for questions.

Years ago, I came down with the flu during the week of our final spring piano party. My first thought was to cancel the event, but our informal parent support group protested and jumped into action. One mom typed the program, and another planned the refreshments; one dad videotaped the performance, while another mom presided as master of ceremonies. One by one, every detail was covered by a student's parent, and the show went on. In this way, the music community extends beyond individual students.

Questions to ponder:

• Did you ever participate in a small group learning experience? As a child? As an adult?

• Did you cooperate in learning together, or did you compete with one another?

• Did you feel safe in making mistakes?

• Was the leader of the group a lecturer or a guide?

• Do your students create a natural music community?

• Do your students' parents and families also create a natural music community?

Did you know?

Bach was the youngest of eight children and came from a musical line which spanned two centuries. His mother died when he was nine years old, and his father died the following year. Bach was raised by an older brother.

Bach taught music, but he did not enjoy teaching and could not tolerate mediocre students. In 1705 in Arnstadt, Bach told a student bassoonist that he sounded like a nanny goat. They began to argue, and Bach drew his dagger to attack him. The student lived, but Bach earned a reputation for not getting along with his students – "wretched" he called them. His genius did not make for a patient, nurturing teacher.

Bach went to work in Liepzig because no better candidates were available. Telemann had been the council's first choice.

J.S. Bach

> *[As a teacher] I possess tremendous power to make a child's life miserable or joyous. I can humiliate or humor, hurt or heal.*
>
> —Haim Ginott

Effective teachers understand the struggles of learning. The most effective teachers have often had personal struggles with the subject they teach. The best math teachers I know struggled with math as children. They understand the road blocks their students experience, and they have a passion for helping them. We have all had teachers who were brilliant in their field of study but were unable to effectively communicate their knowledge to students.

My music education professor once said the following, "Beginners and students who find learning music difficult need the very best teachers. But it is often just the opposite. The best music teachers want the best students. It reflects well on them. Beginners and problem students are often taught by less experienced teachers, sometimes teenagers wanting to earn some extra money." This is backwards.

Most music teachers have not struggled with learning their instrument; otherwise they would not have pursued the field of music as a profession. But each of us can remember the struggle of learning something. What did you struggle with? Reach back into your memory bank and remember that feeling of failure. Did you have an understanding, patient teacher or a frustrated one? Did someone encourage you or discourage you? Did you succeed or give up?

My struggle was with baseball. Having been promoted a grade, I was always the youngest and smallest child in my class. I was able to hold my own until we were out on that dreaded baseball field. I could not catch the ball. I could not hit the ball. I was useless. Nobody wanted me on their team. I still have vivid memories of standing alone on the field as the team captains picked their teams, and I remained the last to be picked. The teachers never tried to instruct me or help me improve my skills. They simply gave up on me. I was hopeless. (Do you have any "hopeless" music students?)

Today, my children are experiencing wonderful physical education programs where building self-esteem and personal improvement are the goals. Their teachers are true educators. That was not the case forty years ago. If baseball was miserable, swimming was even worse! I was fearful of the water and began taking lessons at the community public pool. My teenage teacher thought that making us jump into the deep end would force us to swim. Terrified, I panicked. My teacher became angry and put a pole in the water for me to grab onto. He accidentally hit me on the head with the pole. I survived that awful day, but my fear of the water only grew stronger. Later, I took swimming lessons in a private program with understanding teachers and eventually learned how to swim.

Through all the wonderful music education and piano pedagogy classes I have taken, nothing has helped me more as a teacher than my vivid memories of baseball and swimming. When I am tired after a long day and a piano student continually struggles, I catch my frustration when I remember my own learning experiences. Good teachers see the world through their students' eyes. Our job is to help them, not to condemn or discourage them. We provide a service, and our students and their families are our clients. We are not merely doing them a favor. Parents are entrusting us with their precious children.

As a Suzuki teacher, I believe that talent is a myth. Music making is a developed skill, not a special gift. Realistically, music making is easier for some children than others. One child may have exceptional eye-hand coordination and make rapid progress on the piano. Another child may excel at singing in a choir, while another comfortably plays a brass instrument. The problem begins when we limit music education to those who find it easy.

During the 1950's, this emphasis on talent was prevalent in our school system. Music teachers used standardized testing to evaluate all students for musical talent. The teachers did not realize that such testing simply revealed whether the students had prior music experience. Only the "talented" ones were placed in music education programs. This crime would be no different from giving a child who has not taken a math course a math test or a child who has had no reading experience a reading test and, upon failure of those tests, excluding the child from math or reading programs.

The irony of the music aptitude tests is that the students who evidence home music experience receive more, and students who have not had home music experience receive none.

Questions to Ponder:

What was your greatest learning struggle as a child? As an adult?

What was your teacher's response?

What encouraged or discouraged you?

Now think back to your own music teachers. Making music always came easy to me, but now I realize the reason: I had wonderful teachers. If you are a professional musician, I would imagine that you also had some excellent teachers along the way. These are the educators who shaped the way that you teach today.

I idolized my first teacher. She was patient and kind and made learning to play the piano fun. She was an expert at teaching her students to read music. Her students became excellent sight-readers, with a firm foundation in keys and scales. My second teacher, who taught me during junior high school, introduced me to a wide range of serious literature. Her other expertise was jazz improvisation. I learned how to read a lead sheet and play every imaginable chord. My skills were building one upon another. The ability to sight-read and improvise became bread and butter accompanying jobs all through school. My third teacher, who I enjoyed in high school, was a Juilliard graduate and a very serious musician. She was demanding and dedicated. Her focus was on performing the classics, and she refined my skills. She also coached me as an accompanist and ensemble player. In college and graduate school, I had the privilege of studying with many wonderful piano teachers who carried me beyond "piano acrobatics" and technical proficiency to understanding true musicianship. I treasure each of these teachers for the unique gifts they gave me.

While I was on the waiting list to study with my first teacher, I took lessons with a neighborhood teenage boy. He easily became frustrated with me and hit my hands with a ruler when I made a mistake. In graduate school, I took a course with one professor who enjoyed humiliating students and destroying their confidence. His goal was to "teach us a lesson" and toughen us up. He was not an educator; he was a judge.

Good teachers are constantly asking, "How can I help my students succeed?"

> *In every learning encounter, a teacher asks himself,*
> *"How can I be helpful right now?"*
>
> —Haim Ginott

More Questions:

Take a few minutes to remember your various music teachers in chronological order and list their unique influences on you. What did they each contribute?

What were their teaching styles? Do you have a similar style? What did you emulate and what did you discard?

Did you have any negative influences? How have your negative experiences affected your teaching approach?

I was recently looking for a French horn teacher for my ten-year-old son. My son's passion is baseball, oddly enough, but he has enjoyed studying piano with me and trumpet and French horn in the school band. Mr. Smith (not his real name) came highly recommended. I spoke with Mr. Smith on the phone, explaining that my son was shy and was unsure if he wanted to continue playing the French horn. I thought that having private lessons would help him over the hump. He suggested that we come for a trial lesson.

As a Suzuki teacher, I have always included parents in the music lesson. When we arrived at Mr. Smith's home, he explained that I could sit in on the first lesson, but I would need to wait in the car during future lessons. That should have been my first warning sign.

My quiet, shy son was tentative about meeting Mr. Smith. Twenty minutes into the lesson, Mr. Smith asked my son to make a sound with his voice that he was uncomfortable trying. My son shook his head "no." A good teacher would have said, "Well, let's try that later," or "Let me ask you a different way." A good teacher takes the time to build trust. But Mr. Smith became angry and said, "Then the lesson is over. I don't work with kids who don't do what I ask." I was shocked. At first, I thought he was joking. But he was dead serious. Mr. Smith asked my son one more time to try the exercise, and my son began to cry. I think that Mr. Smith was trying to scare my son into compliance. But I agreed with his initial statement – the lesson was over. My son, in tears, told me that he wanted to leave. This was obviously not a match.

I calmly agreed with Mr. Smith that the lesson was over and wrote a check for his time. He seemed surprised and said, "I guess that I was a little harsh. I was angry. You should have told me on the phone that your son had problems."

The last thing I need in my children's lives is an angry music teacher. The outcome was that my son did not pick up his French horn for months. He decided not to have private lessons. Twenty minutes with a poor, uncaring teacher had catastrophic effects on his desire to make music. Tom McMahon, professor and advocate for children, writes in his column:

> Most children and teens cannot develop self-esteem alone. They need one or more
> people in their lives to nurture it for them, to offer little nudges, one at a time. As

parents, we need to periodically assess our children's support network. It may need tweaking or an overhaul. Every parent has witnessed how one put-down artist can cancel out the influence of 10 other positive people. Remember: the chain of events that can transform your child's self-concept begins with those who surround him.

Whether it is for twenty minutes, or for several weeks, months, or years, music teachers have a powerful influence on their students. We can envelop them in the joy of music making, or we can quickly extinguish any flicker of interest. Since the heart of a child is tender and fragile, we cannot afford to have a bad day at their expense.

One of my daughters had a band teacher who magically connected with his students. He was also my daughter's private flute/oboe teacher while she was a beginner. My daughter and her friend shared a lesson, had weekly music "parties," often came to their lesson dressed in costume, played duets that the teacher composed for them, and celebrated music making in every way. My daughter has graduated to more serious teachers, but she remains passionate about her music.

Months after his traumatic experience, my son began private French horn study with a remarkable young college student who nurtured and encouraged him. I hear beautiful duets and lots of laughter coming from their lessons. He has flourished under her guidance.

We are mentors and music educators first, piano teachers second. Piano study can be the foundation, the introductory piece in the puzzle, which leads to mastering another instrument, whether it be voice, flute, violin, bassoon, cello, trombone, or a host of musical choices. The goal is not to produce professional pianists but to develop human beings who care about others and love to make music.

The question to be asked at the end of an educational step is not, "What has the student learned?" but "What has the student become?"

—James Monroe

More Questions:

If you are a parent, who have been your children's favorite music teachers? How did these teachers inspire and connect with your children?

Do your students look forward to coming to their lessons? Are they disappointed when they miss a lesson?

Does each of your students leave their lessons feeling that they are one of your favorite students? Have they celebrated making music with you? Do you have weekly music parties?

Did you know?

Schubert

Most major composers grew up in musical home environments, where their parents were accomplished musicians. Schubert's father taught him to play the piano and violin. Mozart was coached by his father. Haydn's parents were both amateur musicians, and his father played the harp. Beethoven's father and grandfather were court musicians. Chopin's father played the double bass at the municipal theater.

Strauss

Strauss's father was the first horn player of the the Munich Hofoper. Vivaldi was the son of one of the leading violinists of St. Mark's Chapel. Stravinsky's father was a respected opera singer. J.S. Bach's father was a respected church organist, and all of Bach's sons studied music. Liszt's parents were also amateur musicians. Brahms's father was a double bass player.

> *Engage the learner joyfully and you will get results.*
>
> —Eric Jensen

Children learn when they are engaged. You can see in their faces that they are "with you" and fully participating in the activity at hand. Children do not effectively learn when they are disengaged. Our job as teachers is to engage our students, and this is a challenging task, based on our understanding of how the brain functions.

Cross-modal learning, left-right brain hemisphere, proster theory, the triune brain, the theory of multiple intelligences, neurodevelopmental systems, learning differences, brain-compatible learning – you are probably familiar with these terms. Brain researchers have made many critical contributions to learning theory. As music teachers, it is important to understand what these approaches have in common and how they apply for our students.

Years ago, when I was studying to become a music therapist, cross-modal learning was the focus. Music activities simultaneously targeted auditory, kinesthetic, visual, tactile, cognitive, and social areas. Children's weak areas could be targeted for improvement while employing strong ones. Music making was a cross-over activity, integrating both right and left sides of the brain. Educators and therapists were discovering that each person has a unique learning style and different learning needs do not indicate a lack of intelligence. The burden was no longer on the child to succeed and perform; it became the teacher's job to help the child learn. Music making was the one activity that could reach every child.

The arts develop our imagination in a way that no other life experience can. "Imagination is power," states Dr. Frank Smith. Artists are creators. Creativity is our process for making sense of the world around us, finding solutions to complex problems, and creating new worlds of art. Dr. Smith adds, "Creating is a fundamental and continual urge, and it is a restriction on human potential that so few people do it."

Brain Compatibility

Dr. Leslie Hart has championed developing brain-compatible activities for children in therapy and education. He views linear activities as brain-antagonistic because they do not lead the brain down the path it naturally follows. The brain simultaneously processes along many paths, more complex than our original understanding of left and right hemispheres. Music making connects multiple brain sites.

Dr. Hart describes the brain as a storer of programs. The brain recognizes patterns and chooses the appropriate program to meet the desired goal. The word *proster* derives from program structure. He views the mark of human intelligence as the ability to make plans and carry them out.

Our recognition of patterns and our repertoire of skills necessary to meet new situations rely primarily on our past experience. Dr. Hart defines learning as the capacity to use old programs in fresh combinations. The brain is a pattern-seeking device. The process of learning is adapting and being creative.

Howard Gardner identifies seven intelligences or problem-solving capabilities: verbal/linguistic, logical/mathematical, visual/spatial, body/kinesthetic, musical/rhythmic, interpersonal, and intrapersonal. The more ways children are involved, the more effectively they can learn and adapt. Dr. Mel Levine describes these functions as eight neurodevelopmental systems.

Uniquely Wired Brains

Dr. Levine, a pediatrician and leading expert on how the brain works, describes our minds as tool chests filled with delicate instruments allowing us to learn and perform tasks. These instruments, or neurodevelopmental systems, combine as clusters. The eight systems are attention control, memory, language, motor, higher thinking, social, spatial, and sequential ordering. If you can only read one book about brain functions, read Levine's *A Mind at a Time.*

Dr. Levine compassionately points out that adults rarely have eight equally strong systems. If we are fortunate, we discover our natural bent as adults and find a special niche in life suited to our talents and stronger systems. We learn to compensate for our weaker areas by pursuing strengths, understanding that there is more that is right with us than wrong with us.

Yet if children display weaknesses, educational systems tend to label them and to illuminate their weaknesses under a spotlight. Levine states that each brain is uniquely wired with its own specialized systems and that every human being can benefit from understanding his or her neurodevelopmental profile.

As teachers we need to understand that our efforts are in vain if we do not teach the way the brain learns. More critical, we must adapt our teaching to the way that *individual* brains learn. "Enable them without labeling them," encourages Levine; "Success nourishes motivation and motivation makes further success more likely. Failure dampens motivation and a lack of motivation makes continual failure a near certainty. The neurodevelopmental systems require constant exercise if they are to say in good shape." Feelings of success or failure can be self-fulfilling prophecies. Levine recommends helping children find their unique knack, talent, or creative medium:

> Having a talent can be the wellspring of resiliency. Of course, sometimes hidden talents remain forever hidden and go to waste instead of triggering resiliency. That means parents and teachers have to be on a constant, diligent quest for buried treasure within children.

As a music teacher do you view your job as teaching about mere rhythms and notes or do you view yourself as a mentor who is on a search for buried treasure?

Why Music?

Sound is one of the major sources of brain stimuli that maintains mental vitality. The nucleus basalis is the part of the brain that gives affective meaning to auditory input and codes it in our memory. Music plays a vital role in the development of emotional intelligence and memory storage.

The corpus callosum, the bridge between the left and right sides of the brain, has been found to be thicker in musicians than in non-musicians, suggesting that music may enlarge neural pathways and stimulate learning and creativity. The corpus callosum completes its development by age 11. The cerebellum, the area of the brain involved in rhythm, has also been found to be larger in musicians. Music experience does alter the brain.

Music is a powerful tool in integrating our neurobiological systems. The musical brain is functioning at birth (actually, in the womb during the last three months of development) and continues for a lifetime, making the case for lifelong stimulation and learning. Early music training affects the organization of the musical brain, which consists of neural systems with cognitive, affective, and motor components.

Frank Wilson calls musicians "small muscle athletes" and views learning to play an instrument as the ultimate development of our neurological and motor systems. Dr. Levine includes musical motor output within motor functions, a high-level cluster of muscular responses and sensory imputs. Eric Jensen calls this integration of sensory, cognitive, emotional, and motor capacities the driving force behind all other learning. Music making is the ideal neural networking experience.

The Enemy

> *Teachers often ask psychologists how to motivate children to learn.*
> *The answer is to make it safe for them to risk failure.*
> *To welcome mistakes is to encourage learning.*
>
> —Haim Ginott

The enemies of brain-compatible learning are anxiety and fear. When students feel judged, stressed, or threatened in any way, they cannot learn. Proster theory is based on the triune brain concept. Dr. Paul MacLean described the brain as three partners: the brain stem, the limbic system, and the cerebral cortex. Learning and problem-solving occur in the cerebral cortex. The limbic system connects cognitive and emotional centers. The brain stem is responsible for survival.

Successful problem solving is the ability to adapt and integrate new information with previous experience. When we feel threatened, our brain downshifts to a survival mode, freezing our ability to adapt. We shut down. A stressful performing experience, frustration with an inability to understand a concept or to correctly play a passage, a teacher who is losing patience – these are brain-antagonistic experiences.

Children and adults cannot learn a new skill without taking risks and attempting it anyway. Students who are afraid to make mistakes will not take risks and fearful students cannot learn. Success nourishes motivation, while failure destroys it.

So how do we tangibly put these ideas into practice during music lessons? Here are some concrete suggestions:

1. Remove the words, "No" and "Don't," from your teaching vocabulary. Speak in positives, not negatives. Tell students what you want them to do, not what you do not want them to do. Notice the difference between these statements: "This will sound even better if you slow down a little." vs. "No. Don't rush that. It doesn't sound good."

2. Look for ways to praise students. After a student plays a piece for you, commit to making at least one positive statement before pointing out areas needing improvement. My children's friend told me once that her family's main rule was, "Two put-ups for every put-down." Sometimes it is challenging, but you can find one positive thing to say first. For example, the notes may be right when the rhythms are off; the rhythms may be correct when the notes are wrong; the dynamics and phrasing may be close while the notes and rhythms need help; if everything needs work, perhaps measure 12 was good!

3. Allow students to play pieces in their entirety before offering suggestions and consider it their warm-up. In the spirit of Barry Green's *Inner Game* books, do not interrupt them with constant directions or overwhelm them with a barrage of instructions. This paralyzes the learning process. Offer one suggestion at a time, allowing the student to absorb it and make the correction, before making another suggestion. This is not as critical for older, advanced students, but input should still be limited to two or three suggestions at one time.

4. "Show don't tell" is the rule. Model your suggestions. Music is an aural art. First, demonstrate through playing a passage needing improvement. Second, play with the student.

5. Needless to say, impatience, frustration, or anger have no place in a music lesson. If tension continues with the student (since you may both have a bad day), take an energizer break, a "brain recess," and work on a different piece or discuss another subject. Some old style teachers believe that their obvious disapproval motivates students to practice and to never come to a lesson unprepared. While this may work with some students, it comes at a very high price and may even lead some students to quit.

When students appear unprepared, they may actually be struggling with the assigned task. It is our job to help them overcome the obstacles and be successful. If students consistently come to lessons unprepared and are not practicing, this reflects a motivation problem. Then we need to ask ourselves some questions, "Why is this student bored? Is the music interesting? Are the pieces too challenging or not challenging enough? How can I make music making relevant in their lives?" Perhaps playing the piano is not the best fit for the student's neurodevelopmental profile. Excelling on the piano requires a high level of fine-motor/eye-hand coordination. A child may struggle with learning to play the piano yet have the capability to be a outstanding musician on another instrument. We are music educators first, and piano teachers second.

Those pesky SAT Scores

> *Musical intelligence and achievement is its own reward, as seen countless times in our students.*
>
> —Steve Demorest & Steve Morrison

You have probably read it in countless professional journals, popular magazines, and books about music and the brain. We are bombarded with findings: Language and math skills improve with music training; rhythm activities with young children improve reading; music lessons make kids smarter; music experience improves spatial skills; music training increases SAT scores. In fact, the American Music Conference in 1997 announced that piano instruction improved reasoning skills in math and science.

Don Campbell, in *Introduction to the Musical Brain*, claimed that music stimulation increased intelligence. His popular book, *The Mozart Effect*, made research about the impact of music on human development accessible to the public. His information has become common knowledge, easing the battle that music therapists and music educators have in defending music budgets and the importance of music programs, and trying to convince parents and administrators that music training benefits the whole individual.

However, I agree with opponents that this pendulum has swung too far. Even though music education increases SAT scores, the question is becoming, "So what?" Do SAT tests accurately test a student's intelligence, potential, and capabilities? No. That is why some colleges are now moving away from requiring the test for admission. Standardized tests are linear, left-brain experiences. Do they "measure" creativity and artistic abilities? No. The stress of taking tests is certainly brain-antagonistic. Should the reason a child studies music hinge on increased SAT scores? No! Do we need to listen to Mozart and other serious literature because it will accelerate our learning? Must musical experiences always be validated with extramusical benefits? No! Testing reflects our culture's obsession with visible productivity. We can listen to or play beautiful music simply because it touches a deep place in our soul. We do not need to justify our reasons for enjoying the arts by higher test scores.

Current researchers caution teachers to be wary. They warn that many studies have found music experience and increased skills in other areas to be correlated but not necessarily causal. Imagine placing students in rigorous mathematics programs so that they can become better musicians. Ralph Spingte says the following, "'Music makes you smarter' is an exaggeration that is disastrous to the field of music medicine, because this statement is perceived by the public as 'just listen to music and you get smarter.' That is nonsense. However, music can enhance attention, focus, and motivation, and should be part of every general education experience."

Eric Jensen warns educators that the arts are not merely a quick fix for low test scores. Arts experiences change the brain slowly over time. The value lies in lasting results. He points out that character building and nurturing relationships are equally "inefficient." Jensen states that our goal should not be higher test scores, but our top priority should be better human beings – creative, compassionate, confident, feeling, and thinking individuals who are passionate about learning and can relate well to others. In a culture where technology is highly prized, the arts are still what make us human.

Guess what another equally strong predictor of success in testing and college achievement is? Eating dinner as a family. The message is not to teach during the dinner hour for the sake of your students' families and your own family. Family is the most important community.

Nevertheless, there is no question that music listening and experience uniquely affects the entire development of a human being. That has been proven. We now need a more balanced approach. Music making has added benefits, but the main reason that we teach children to play instruments is for them to experience making beautiful music, which will bring unparalleled joy for a lifetime. Making music with other people is an especially rewarding experience.

> *Art is the signature of civilization.*
> —Beverly Sills

In Summary:

1. The common thread found in decades of research is that effective education is brain-compatible, with activities designed to take the brain down many paths simultaneously, integrate multiple intelligences, and connect brain sites.

2. Every human brain is uniquely wired, with some strong neurodevelopmental systems and some weaker ones. Our job as teachers is to teach the way individual brains learn and to help students strengthen their specialized systems and improve their weaker ones.

3. Music making is a natural brain-compatible process and the ideal neural networker. Music engages all our capabilities in one process. In addition to acquiring musical skills, music making also benefits students in other areas of their development.

4. The arts are powerful guides to tapping our imaginations and the urge to be creative.

5. Brain-antagonistic experiences cause the brain to downshift. Fear and stress can cause students to shut down. Linear activities that target only one of the multiple intelligences may cause students to disengage. Neither boredom or anxiety help children learn.

Questions to Ponder:

What is your individual learning style? How is your brain uniquely wired? What are your strong neurodevelopmental systems? Are you a visual, auditory, or tactile/kinesthetic learner? What are your weaker or stronger modes? Are you left- or right-brain dominant?

Do you remember a stressful experience when your brain shut down? Do you remember a concert or performance when your brain shut down?

Observe two of your students: What are their learning styles? Their strengths? When are they engaged? When do you seem to lose their attention?

If you have children, apply these questions to them as well.

Give each new student a family questionnaire to be filled out by parents, with questions about the student's learning style, the family's musical background and tastes, the child's birth date, and other information.

> Did you know that the strongest brain connector is humor? We most effectively learn when we laugh. We laugh when we are fully engaged. We also remember what we learned when we laughed in the process. Think back over the speakers you have recently heard. What information do you remember? It is probably connected with laughter. Humor is a powerful teacher, the ultimate brain-compatible experience. Laughter changes the chemicals in our body. Victor Borge said, "Humor is the shortest distance between two people."

Did you know?

Verdi

Berlioz, Schumann, Rimsky-Korsakov, Verdi, and Wagner did not grow up in musical families. The great composer Wagner could not play the piano. Neither Berlioz nor Wagner ever learned to correctly play an instrument. When Rimsky-Korsakov became professor of composition at St. Petersburg Conservatory, he lay awake at night worrying because he did not even have a basic background in music theory. He and Borodin had learned about instrumentation by spending weekends experimenting and playing a variety of instruments together. When Verdi applied to the conservatory in Milan, he was rejected because he had insufficient music training. Dvořák was not well-educated and was barely more than literate. His only interest outside of music was trains.

Suzuki, Orff, Kodály, and Dalcroze: Applications for Cooperative Learning and Inclusion

> *In teaching, you will come to grief as soon*
> *as you forget that your pupils have bodies.*
>
> —Alfred North Whitehead
> The Aims of Education, 1929

The Suzuki, Orff-Schulwerk, Kodály, and Dalcroze Methods are perfect compliments to any group class program. Each approach is uniquely brain compatible and celebrates cooperative learning. As a music therapist, it was natural for me to integrate Orff activities into my Suzuki teaching. I have also had the privilege of observing my own children and students with Kodály and Dalcroze instructors. I have been amazed at the similarities in the methods and applaud the complimentary differences. In the true spirit of cooperative learning, teachers of the four methods can model cooperation vs. competition. No one method is better than another; this is not a contest.

We can pool our skills to provide the best music education program possible for each of our students, depending on their individual needs and learning styles. Good teachers synthesize different approaches in the best interest of the child. We can focus on the positive, build on students' strengths, and help them improve their weaknesses.

One time a friend shared with me that she had a dilemma. She took her daughter one afternoon a week to a Suzuki piano teacher for Suzuki lessons, and on another afternoon during the week she took her to a traditional piano teacher to learn to read music and study supplementary materials. How could this happen? Parents and students also need to understand all the current methods.

An overview of each of these methods follows. Note the principles which support inclusion, cooperative learning, and brain compatibility theory. Become aware of the similarities between the Suzuki, Orff, Kodály, and Dalcroze Methods and their application to students with special needs.

The Suzuki Method

Shinichi Suzuki (1898-1998)

© Arthur Montzka

> *"Talent Education" does not only apply to knowledge or technical skill but*
> *also to morality, building character, and appreciating beauty.... Our movement*
> *does not mean to raise prodigies. We must express it in other words as "total*
> *human education" or "enriched environment."*
>
> —Masaaki Honda

It is easy to see why the Suzuki Method is often misunderstood. Young Suzuki students are sometimes viewed as prodigies with a regimented lifestyle, immersed in a method for gifted children. Non-Suzuki teachers point out that Suzuki students cannot read music, and some parents are concerned that the method is limited. But these criticisms entirely misunderstand Suzuki's intention.

Sometimes untrained Suzuki teachers misunderstand the method. They become more focused on the Suzuki book literature and recordings than on the core philosophy. Shinichi Suzuki was an unusually creative educator, who instinctively knew how the brain functioned. The idea behind Book 1 is that students are learning familiar songs in their culture. When students are not familiar with these songs, it is the teacher's job to find folk songs that they are familiar with. We must think outside of the box, for Suzuki certainly did. Advanced students who are studying Beethoven's sonatas, Chopin's nocturnes, or Bartok's *Mikrokosmos* should be listening to recordings of those works.

Dr. Suzuki developed his method in Japan while working with exceptional children and young people who had been traumatized during World War II. The Suzuki Method is founded on the mother tongue concept. Suzuki observed that all children immersed in their language since birth learn to expertly speak their native tongue. Suzuki spent his life demonstrating that similar immersion in a musical home environment develops an equal fluency in music. Suzuki has exposed the myth of "talent." Talent is not a gift but an ability that can be developed in the proper environment, hence the terms "ability development", or "talent education."

Suzuki music making is a product of listening and experience, not of matching notes on a page. Pieces are taught by imitation. Suzuki believed that teaching a child to read music before the child can play it is analogous to teaching a child to read before he or she can speak. Symbols cannot be associated with a process one has never experienced. Music reading should be postponed until after the child's musical skills are established.

Born in Nagoya, Japan, Suzuki grew up as the son of a violin maker in a musical family. He began seriously studying the violin at age seventeen and rapidly progressed. At age twenty-three, he went to Germany to study with Karl Klinger and was influenced by Western music and culture. He began working with young children and developing his own philosophy in 1931. Prompted by his desire to bring healing to children devastated in World War II, Suzuki opened the Matsumoto Talent Education School in 1945. The school quickly grew. It is still flourishing, and offers musical instruction in various instruments, art, calligraphy, English, gymnastics, and math – all employing the Suzuki approach.

Suzuki values the human potential of any individual and believes that there are no failures. Though it is never too late to begin the Suzuki process, the method is based on starting children as early as possible. Suzuki developed a listening environment program for infants. Children begin formal individual and group music lessons on an instrument during the preschool years and continue the process as a way of life. Suzuki followers emphasize it is not only a music education method but also an approach to living.

Critics of the Suzuki Method have charged Suzuki with turning out young robot prodigies, but close examination of his method shows that this was never his intention. Suzuki's conviction is that a musical life is an enriched, full, and happier life. He was committed to the well-being of the whole child. Two well-known statements by Suzuki embody his philosophy: "Where love is deep, much can be accomplished" and "Character first, ability second." Suzuki believed that a highly developed musical intellect and sensitivity are transferred to all areas of life, citing Einstein as a prime example.

Critics see young violinists playing Vivaldi concertos and do not understand Suzuki's role in special education. He understood the process of music making to be therapeutic. He attributed his success with exceptional children to sheer persistence and practice. In his work with the physically impaired, he discovered that physical limitations improved as a result of making music. Following his example, Suzuki teachers have effectively taught music making to the visually impaired, learning disabled, chronically ill, developmentally disabled, individuals with cerebral palsy, and the aging.

The basic principles of the Suzuki Method do not change when applied to the exceptional. Teachers adapt by moving at a slower pace, requiring more repetitions and breaking the tasks down into the smallest parts possible. Realistically, exceptional students may not even reach the intermediate to advanced literature.

However, students who are visually impaired or intellectually unable to read are fully able to participate in the Suzuki Method. It provides an excellent preparation for blind students to learn Braille music. Suzuki's life approach to developing a music making ability in any individual, regardless of age or ability, provides evidence that he did not conceive of music therapy and music education as separate fields, but as extensions of one another.

Learning to make music on an instrument is one of the most complex tasks an individual can approach. It involves all the perceptual, cognitive, and kinesthetic processes simultaneously and is the highest integration of developmental skills. Learning to play an instrument can be a highly therapeutic process, and students are motivated by the high quality product. They can make real music. The Suzuki Method has proven to be effective with all ages and abilities. Applicable to the exceptionally limited as well as the gifted, it is ideal for mainstreaming. The same method can be used with all students by varying the individual pace in a classroom, in a group, or in a private setting. The basic principles of the Suzuki Method follow:

1. Music education begins at birth. Children are exposed daily to high quality music in their environment, including cultural folk songs as well as serious art music.

2. Students begin study on an instrument during the preschool years. They learn by imitating the teacher and listening daily to recordings of songs they are learning. Music making is play. Beginning students learn familiar childhood folk songs. Children's ears are their best teachers. The Suzuki repertoire is contained in a carefully sequenced set of books with corresponding recordings adapted for each instrument. Daily listening accelerates the process and most closely parallels how we learn our native tongue.

3. The Suzuki Method starts with life experience and returns to it. Experiences familiar to the student are used to teach musical principles, and the accomplishment transfers to other skill areas. For example, the first pieces learned in Suzuki *Book I* for all instruments are the "Twinkle, Twinkle Little Star Variations." The rhythmic variations on this familiar folk song encompass all basic aspects of technique and musicality and form the foundation of the method. The rhythms are ideally taught first through speech patterns, clapping, moving, playing rhythm instruments, and finally transferring to the studied instrument. Speech patterns of food names such as pepperoni pizza are often used because food is common to everyone's experience.

4. The greatest criticism of the Suzuki Method has been that students do not learn to read music until it is too late. Suzuki never intended to produce non-reading musicians. He wanted students to start music study early enough to have had those musical experiences before learning to read music. It is the music teacher's job to provide supplementary reading methods at the proper level.

5. Ability breeds ability. Each Suzuki piece and technique builds upon previous pieces. The method moves the child in small steps that can be easily mastered. Students set their own pace.

6. Constant repetition is the key to mastery. Previous pieces in the Suzuki books are consistently reviewed. Students know their repertoire so well that written music is not needed and performance for others is natural and joyful. Upon completion of Suzuki *Book I*, students give a *Book I* recital where they play their entire repertoire.

7. The Suzuki Method focuses on the total well-being and self-esteem of children, not on their musical product. Learning blocks occur as the result of criticism or pressure. The Suzuki teacher provides a safe and joyful learning environment in which students are affirmed for what is done right and are not criticized. The parents are taught to provide the same environment at home, and siblings are welcome to participate in the music process. The Suzuki Method involves one success experience built on another.

8. This is a family method. The parent is the home teacher. The parent attends all lessons, takes notes, and receives instruction. If not already a musician, the parent will become one! In the Suzuki Method, it is never too late or too early to learn. The parent works with the child daily at home. The teacher, student, and parent form the Suzuki "triangle."

9. The Suzuki program is a group experience. Students have private sessions with their teacher and also attend group classes to make music with other students. An attitude of cooperation (vs. competition) and of helping one another is fostered. Music making is the tool for developing positive social skills.

**Carl Orff
(1895-1982)**

The Orff-Schulwerk Method

Orff-Schulwerk was developed by the German composer Carl Orff (1895-1982). Orff never set out to develop one of the most innovative music education/therapy approaches of our century. His initial dream was to effectively integrate music and dance for the theater. His work with Dorothea Gunther, a trainer of dancers and gymnasts, eventually evolved into his Schulwerk, or school work.

Orff observed that children experience music, movement, and speech (songs, chants) simultaneously in their play. This natural process of music making he termed "elemental." Orff believed that children should be taught music as they naturally experience it, through an integration of music, speech, movement, and childhood chants.

The Orff-Schulwerk Method begins with the person and the creative process, not a desired musical product. The Orff experience is spontaneous and unplanned. The children create it. Orff believed that rhythm was central to music making and should be developed in early childhood. The process begins with materials of the child's world, such as the rhythm of his or her own name.

Orff-Schulwerk is rooted in exploration and creative experience. It is a method of play, which we know to be the child's "work." Orff students explore space through movement, and explore sound through speech, song, instruments, and patterns of music (form). This method is consistent with the idea that the brain is a pattern-seeking device and learns by associations. Children begin by imitating the Orff leader and then move to improvising their own creations. They work as a community, an ensemble.

Unique to Orff-Schulwerk are the Orff instruments, influenced by Orff's exposure to African and Indonesian music. The Orff instrumentarium is easily accessible to children of various abilities and offers a variety of timbres and textures, including cymbals, drums, glockenspiels, xylophones, metallophones, recorders, strings, and other folk instruments. Children progress from making music with their bodies (snapping, clapping, stomping) to improvising music on complex instruments. Orchestral instruments are also used.

Musical elements in the beginning Orff process are as follows:

1. The pentatonic mode. This scale without the fourth and fifth tones is the source of all childhood folk songs. The minor third is universally central to children's songs.

2. Ostinato patterns and the development of motives.

3. Simple forms, such as canon and rondo.

4. Children's materials/songs from their own culture.

5. Creative dramatics, poetry, and story literature to develop music dramas at the child's level.

Advanced Orff-Schulwerk incorporates complex harmonies, mixed meters, modes, music forms and dance forms that lead participants to a mastery of improvisatory composition skills. Orff-Schulwerk is that unique magical process that taps every creative facet of one's being. Orff-Schulwerk can be as simple as a developmentally disabled child playing the rhythm of his or her name on a drum or a group of emotionally disturbed adolescents expressing their emotions through creating a composition, or as complex as advanced students creating an Orff "symphony."

The Kodály Method

© Photo by István Harmath (1966)

**Zoltan Kodály
(1882-1967)**

Zoltan Kodály (1882-1967) developed a comprehensive music education program in the Hungarian school system. Today it is recognized worldwide as the Kodály Method and is based on the following principles:

1. Kodály believed that all people can become as musically literate as they are language literate. Reading and writing music should be as natural for children as reading and writing their native language. Kodály viewed music as a core subject to be taught daily in the classroom on a level with academic subjects. Today reading specialists view rhythm skills as a key factor in teaching reading.

2. The natural activity of singing is the basis for teaching musicianship, hence the term "choral musicianship." The singing process is accessible to all and is immediately internalized. Song materials should come from the folk song repertoire of the child's own culture.

3. To be most effective, music education must begin with the very young child.

4. Children should be exposed to the highest quality music, from folk songs to serious art music. Aesthetic sensitivity is a developed awareness. We are not simply born with a discerning taste for good art.

Kodály based his systematic method on the natural progression of developmental skills in children. For example, all children throughout the world sing their earliest songs on the minor third interval in duple rhythm. What child does not tease others with "na-ni, na-ni, na-ni, can't catch me!" using those intervals?

As children grow, they naturally include more intervals of the scale and more complex rhythms in their song literature. Kodály developed a carefully sequenced approach that taught children musical skills in the order they were ready for them. He incorporated movement and folk dance as extensions of singing.

Kodály employed the established sight-singing tool, sol-fa, to teach music reading. He combined that system with hand signals, which originated with John Curwen in England. Each sol-fa syllable corresponds with a specific hand signal that reinforces tonal memory. Rhythmic durations are also assigned syllabic patterns (such as ta, ti-ti).

Developing musical memory and inner hearing are other vital aspects of the Kodály Method. Children are taught to hear songs internally. Students do not begin instrument study until they have first mastered Kodály choral skills.

The Dalcroze Method

What the singing voice is to the Kodály Method, the natural rhythmic movement responses of the human body are to the Dalcroze Method.

Emile Jaques-Dalcroze (1865-1950) viewed movement as the method for internalizing musicianship skills. His method, termed eurhythmics, had has an impact on music education, as well as on dance and therapy.

While Dalcroze was a professor at the Conservatory of Music in Geneva, he found that his students, though exceptionally advanced on their instruments, could not master the simplest rhythms. He further discovered that while they could not play in tempo, his pupils could easily walk in tempo. The students could not feel the flow of a musical phrase while playing their instruments, yet their muscles tensed at the height of the phrase and relaxed at the end. Although natural music making was in their bodies, it did not transfer to their playing. As a result, Dalcroze developed an individual system of rhythmic movement exercises based on the following principles:

1. Rhythm is the basic element of music.

2. Rhythm is motion. All rhythms in music have their roots in the natural rhythm of the human body and can be experienced in movement.

3. Our bodies are our first instruments. We cannot play music that we cannot first feel through movement.

Eurhythmics is not to be confused with dance. Eurhythmics focuses on our kinesthetic sense, that link between experiential movement and cognitive processing. Today therapists and educators are well aware of the role of the kinesthetic sense in helping clients and students.

Dalcroze's movement repertoire consists of movements in place and movements in space. Different combinations of movements comprise the exercises as students respond to musical changes. The preparation for the movement and the relaxation after the movement are as important rhythmically as the action itself.

The Dalcroze teacher improvises music at the piano, combining different elements of rhythm and including "surprises" for the students' responses. Exercises proceed from simple walking and clapping for the youngest students to the most complex rhythmic problems for advanced students.

Eurhythmics is the hallmark of the Dalcroze Method but the method actually consists of three parts:

1. Rhythmic movement.

2. Solfege singing (similar to the sol-fa singing used in the Kodály Method). The development of inner hearing and memory are crucial.

3. Improvisation. Through movement, speech, song, and instruments, students are expected to spontaneously create and play at music making as opposed to being mechanically tied to written notes on a page. Dalcroze's goal was for his students to experience the same freedom on their instruments that they experienced in movement.

Dalcroze viewed musicianship as the integration of inner hearing, inner muscular response, and creative expression. Attending to our kinesthetic sense is a learned process.

Synthesis

Though their techniques vary, the philosophies of Dalcroze, Kodály, Suzuki, and Orff are remarkably similar. What is critically important for music teachers to realize is what these four methods have in common and how we can integrate these principles into our program:

1. Children should have music experiences as young as possible. All people can become as musically literate as they are language literate. Talent is a myth.

2. Through experience, singing, movement, and listening, children can internalize musicianship skills before moving on to apply them to instrument study.

3. Music experience must precede music reading. Inner hearing of what one plays must precede actually playing it on an instrument.

4. Children should be exposed to the highest quality of music materials, from the folk songs of their culture to serious music.

5. Comprehensive (well-rounded) musicianship is the goal. Developing musical sensitivity and understanding the nuances of phrasing, dynamics, etc. are inherent in each method.

6. A cooperative spirit of ensemble music making is encouraged. Competition has no place.

7. Children should be taught music in the way they naturally experience, through movement, listening, chant/song, and instrument experimentation. Pedgogical material should come from the child's own world.

8. Rhythm is the source of all music experience. Melody grows out of rhythm.

9. The music experience is a process, and the goal is the well-being of the student. The goal is never a musical product. An appreciation for music develops finer human beings. Music making is a gift of lifetime joy.

Did you know?

Mendelssohn

Mendelssohn came from a strict and loving family. He was a prodigy equally as talented as Mozart, but his parents did not want to exploit him. They protected him from fame and made his education a priority. Mendelssohn and his sister, Fanny, enjoyed playing duo piano works as children and remained close friends throughout their lives.

Scott Joplin

Scott Joplin's father moved out and abandoned his family because he was furious that Scott wanted to pursue music.

> *When music teachers teach, they simultaneously perform. We make music with our students. I cannot think of another subject area in which the roles of the teacher and students are so intertwined.*
>
> —Richard Kennell

The inspiration for a group class can be any theme or topic chosen to be studied. This is a brainstorming chapter. The ideas are not organized into categories – the curse of creativity. Our planning process should be brain-compatible. I want you to experience free-flowing ideas, one tumbling from another, without judgment. Keep a journal handy to write down your own ideas. We will organize the ideas into plans (linear thinking) in the following chapter.

Mindmapping, the whole brain planning process, was developed by Tony Buzan in the 1970s. It immediately became popular in the business world and is now applied to many other fields as well. Mindmapping is a brainstorming process involving our whole brain in which we "dump out" all our information and ideas without analysis and judgment. Analysis and judgment paralyze creativity and innovation. Mindmappers work alone or in groups. They simply let the ideas flow, amazed at the associations that appear and new solutions that surface when blocks are removed. Mindmaps are as individual as the people using them. Mindmaps are tools.

Mindmapping begins with a central focus (the center cloud on a piece of paper) and proceeds by brainstorming all the possible approaches and solutions (the webs emanating from the center). Key words, images, drawings, and the use of different colored pens help in the process. Mindmappers often listen to music to enhance free flow creativity.

We can mindmap/brainstorm group class plans alone, with other teachers, or with our students. The following ideas began as a mindmap and are written here for easier reading. Try experimenting with mindmaps as you jot down your own inspirations.

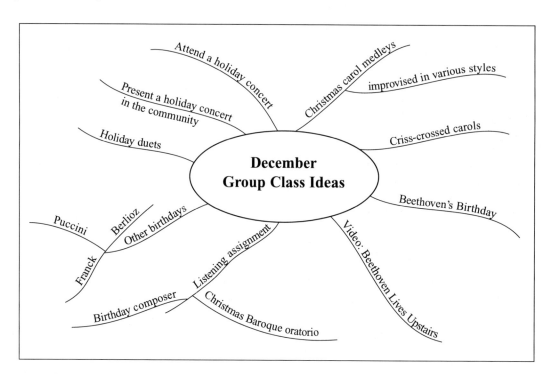

Ideas for Piano Group Class

Introduce students to a different instrument family at each group class: winds, strings, brass, and percussion. Explain the instruments in each family and invite a guest performer to demonstrate his or her instrument. Siblings or parents may be the perfect resource. Pianists need to understand how other instruments work in order to accompany them.

Introduce students to a different period of music at each group class. Students are given a listening assignment. For example, "Listen to a work by a Baroque composer and come prepared to discuss it with us."

Have an "Accompanying" class where students come prepared to accompany an instrumentalist or vocalist of their choice. The guest soloist can be a family member or friend.

Assign students an expert report on a composer of their choice. They will present the history of the composer and selected works. The composer's birthday is an ideal time to present an expert report.

Especially fun is the "Tonight Show" format. Students take on the role of their composers and prepare scripts. Another student interviews the artist about his or her life and current works, including a performance by the artist. Students can make this experience quite funny and entertaining.

Have a "Composition" class where students share their original works or an improvisation class where students learn to spontaneously create their own music.

Have an "Orchestration" class where students select one of their compositions to orchestrate. Encourage family members to participate in the music making. Younger students may orchestrate a short composition with drums, maracas, and clapping. Older students may develop complex works which require serious rehearsal, including a variety of orchestral instruments. They can learn to write the score for their works.

Encourage younger students to create "name symphonies" using the rhythms in their names.

A "Transposition" class can be fun and challenging. Students can practice transposing their pieces into other keys and modes. Especially effective at the October group class is transposing pieces into a minor key.

Have a "Theme and Variations" class where each student prepares his or her own rendition of the same song. This is an excellent way to teach musical styles. At holiday group class, students enjoy preparing different versions of the same Christmas carol.

Have a "Prelude in C by J.S. Bach" class. After having studied the original and analyzed the harmonies, each student offers a variation based on the chords. This assignment can include learning to write a lead sheet.

"Playing in the Round" is a fun activity if you have more than one piano in your studio. Select a simple round (e.g. "Row Your Boat") and have students first sing the round, and then play it as they rotate through the pianos. Advance to more complex rounds. A little improvisation adds great fun.

In honor of April Fool's Day, plan a Victor Borge class, where students have the opportunity to add some comedy to their performances. Victor Borge videos are available for those students who are unfamiliar with his work.

Have a "Disney" class, or a musical class, or a movie class, or a TV theme class to give students the opportunity to play their favorite popular pieces.

"Criss-Crossed Carols" is a fun game that we've played as a family which has been challenging for Christmas group class. The students are divided into teams, and the goal is to sing the lyrics of one Christmas carol to the tune of another. It is very difficult! They pull slips of paper out of jars to find they may be singing "Frosty the Snowman" lyrics to the tune of "Silent Night" or "Away in the Manger" lyrics to the tune of "Jingle Bells". This activity requires incredible focus.

Study ABA form by encouraging students to create their own ABA compositions, transposing from major (A) to minor (B). Young students can arrange folk songs, such as "Row Your Boat" or "Mary Had a Little Lamb", in ABA form. Older students can base their arrangements on original melodies.

Celebrate composers' birthdays throughout the year, complete with all the party trimmings and a birthday cake. Beethoven's birthday, December 16, is a great opportunity for a Christmas/birthday party. In addition to holiday literature, each student can play a piece by Beethoven and listen to one of his works. Students share the most interesting fact they learned about him.

Assign students a different genre of music to listen to each month – chamber music, choral works, opera, symphonies, etc.

Use your time as students arrive for group class. Have a recording playing in the background that is relevant to the group class topic. Can the students guess what it is? Have the students write down their responses, place them in a jar, and have a raffle drawing of the correct responses at the end of class.

To learn musical terms, dates, and more, alert students that there will be a "password" posted on the door. They can only enter group class if they know the definition.

Incorporate learning a new instrument, such as the recorder or the guitar, into group class.

"Magic Music" is a wonderful game for teaching dynamics to young children. Ask one student to leave the room and hide a small rhythm instrument. When the student returns to find it, the other students start singing. The closer the student gets to the instrument, the louder the students sing, and the farther away, the softer they sing.

Introduce students to sol-feg and sight-singing. Invite a Kodály specialist to visit one of your group classes or arrange a summer workshop in your studio.

Invite a visiting Orff or Dalcroze specialist to work with your students. What they learn through playing Orff instruments and moving their bodies cannot be duplicated at the piano.

Plan an "Introduction to Jazz" class, complete with listening assignments. Plan a year to monthly study the evolution of jazz from its roots to the present day.

Using letter tiles and an egg timer, divide the students into groups and see how many music terms, composers' names, etc. they can make in three minutes. One variation is using the letters of first names to make an acrostic of composers and terms.

Plan a "choral class", encouraging students to bring a choral piece, as simple as a song or hymn or an actual choral work. Students practice accompanying the "choir" of other students and family members.

Offer an "Introduction to Opera" class. Ask students to read one of the famous opera stories.

Encourage students to keep a journal of works they have listened to and their reactions. Have students write letters to their favorite composers or reviews of their works.

Discuss a different musical form at each group class. Create an Orff game to teach the rondo form and progress to more complex forms.

Explore published variations and assign one or two variations to each student, performing the entire work at a special group class. Mozart's "Twinkle Little Star" is an obvious choice, especially for incorporating Suzuki beginners who are learning "Twinkle Variations" with more advanced students. A few of my personal favorites are as follows:

1. *Variations on Happy Birthday from Bach to Boogie* by Denes Agay (a perfect resource for celebrating students' birthdays). Styles include neo-Bach, Mozart, Beethoven, Schubert, Chopin, Liszt, Strauss, John Philip Sousa, Debussy, Gershwin, Boogie.
2. *The Chopsticks Variations* by Margo Guryan. Movements include Round, Andante, Allegretto, Rhymes, Andantino, Ragtime, Boogie Woogie, Inventionette, Adagio, Allegro, Barcarole, Walking, Melody, Finale.
3. *Happy Birthday, Dear Ludwig* by Leonard Hambro (in the style of Beethoven.)
4. *Happy Birthday, in Style* by Eugenie Rocherolle (styles include classical, rag and Gershwin.)

Plan a "Scale Extravaganza" class where students come prepared to play an original composition based on a variety of scales played in different ways: contrary motion, in parallel thirds, sixths, tenths, major/minor, etc. A similar arpeggio class is fun. Any technique can be explored in a composition.

Encourage students to attend one live music event every few months and then write a review. A student newsletter, including the reviews and other group class news is a fun project. Plan a field trip for group class to attend a concert together.

Encourage students to listen to a different piano concerto from a different period each month and to attend one live performance of a piano concerto during the year.

The following year, encourage students to listen to a flute concerto one month, a violin concerto the next, a cello concerto the third month, and to then continue through their favorite instruments.

Students can compare and contrast two composers by listening to their respective works. The assignment would be "Tell me three ways that the composers are similar and three ways that they are different." Students should be encouraged to bring visual aids, which always help other students to focus during the presentations to group class.

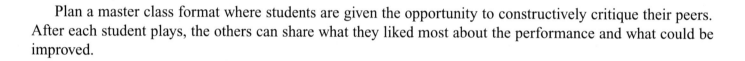

If students are struggling with finding time to complete their listening assignments, use part of group class to listen to key works while playing musical chairs.

Encourage your students to participate in community service. Take your students to a local senior center to perform.

Play "Name That Tune" at the year's final group class, incorporating all the listening assignments.

Plan a master class format where students are given the opportunity to constructively critique their peers. After each student plays, the others can share what they liked most about the performance and what could be improved.

Play a musical version of the popular alphabet car game. Going around the circle, starting with the letter "A" and continuing through the alphabet, each student says, "I'm traveling on a musical journey and I am taking _____." The trick is to recite in order all the previous musical terms or composers' names, etc. This is a challenging auditory memory game.

Capitalize on holidays with love songs at Valentine's Day, hymns at Thanksgiving, or whatever songs celebrate the culture and traditions of your individual students. Hymns are an excellent tool for teaching four-part harmony.

Have an "Ostinato Bass" class, where each student composes a bass line and other students lay parts over it. Orff instruments are helpful for this activity.

Plan a musical game party, where each student presents a musical game that he or she created. Adaptations of popular party games, like "Balderdash" or "Outburst", make for a great piano party.

"TV Game Show" class is a fun way to teach musical concepts and history. "Jeopardy", "Family Feud", "Password" and others can be adapted to music topics.

Play "Composer Botticelli." "Botticelli" is a version of twenty questions about a famous person. Students can ask up to twenty questions about the composer to guess his or her identity. Pinning pieces of paper with composers' names on the backs of students when they arrive for group class is another fun way to challenge them to remember facts about the composers' lives. Students ask each other questions to guess their own identity.

Each student selects one composer's music to be immersed in during the year. For example, if the student selects Mozart, the first month he or she will listen to a symphony; the next month, a piano sonata; then a choral work, then a chamber work, etc. The student can prepare an "expert report" on that composer to share with group class.

For younger students, plan a "Change the Piece" class. Students pick cards out of a jar giving them instructions on how to change their prepared piece: change the dynamics, tempo, key, articulation, and more.

Plan a "Medley" class, where students play medleys of similar songs they have arranged, complete with bridges. Christmas carols, movie themes, and jazz tunes make for ideal medleys. One approach is to combine different songs. The other is to combine different versions of the same song, changing keys (major/minor) and styles.

Have a "Duet Group" class that can include duets at one piano, duo piano works, or eight hands at two pianos. A theme duet class is fun, celebrating holiday duets, Mozart's duets, Schubert's duets, or others. (Refer to *Music for the Piano* by Friskin and Freundlich for a listing by composer.)

Have a "Family Ensemble" class, where the students arrange one of their pieces to be played with members of their family accompanying on a variety of instruments.

Plan a "Silly Song" class, where students can compose or play published silly songs. The lyrics are the best part.

Play auditory bingo with musical works, instruments, rhythms, or musical terms.

Have students choose a favorite poem or write one and create music to match it. Jack Preletksy's holiday poem books are a wonderful resource.

Have a "Clef and Score Reading" class for advanced students, focusing on the alto and tenor clefs.

Rotating through easy duets is a fun and effective way to have a "Sight-reading" class.

Play "Twister," where students match rhythms instead of colors. They can first match them visually, and then only by listening.

Have a voice teacher come to explain how the voice works as an instrument.

For very advanced students, arrange a "Concerto" class, where other students play the reduced orchestral parts.

Have an "Early Music" class, where students can play keyboard works from the *Fitzwilliam Virginal Book* or works by Couperin or Rameau. Encourage students to attend in costume!

Students are assigned an "arts overview" for one period of music or composer. They discuss art, dance, drama, and literature relevant to the period.

Have a class which focuses on women composers or the children of famous composers (e.g., J.S. Bach's sons).

Have an "Invention" class, or a "Minuet" class, or a "Sonatina" class, or a "Boogie" class, or a "Mozart" class, or a "Debussy" class – the possibilities are endless for celebrating your students' learning of new literature.

More crazy ideas for the most adventurous:

What about hosting a tea for salon music? Or an English tea for Handel's birthday? Or creating a dinner club environment with small tables around the room to perform jazz pieces?

What about having a musical scavenger hunt in your neighborhood?

What about a progressive group class where students play different types of literature at a few select students' homes – moving from appetizers to desserts?

Your Turn

Did you know?

Chopin supported himself in elegant style through private teaching. He enjoyed having wealthy students of aristocratic society. Chopin published his first piece at age eight. His composition teacher, Joseph Elsner, never forced Chopin to copy other styles but encouraged him to naturally develop his own style.

Chopin

Students from all over Europe came to study with Liszt in Weimar. He was a showman, and a powerful entertainer, with an ego to match his skills. Liszt invented the solo piano recital. Women were easily attracted to him, and Liszt was involved in scandalous affairs.

Liszt

Building on the ideas from the previous chapter, let's now brainstorm further about some unique additions.

Composers' Birthday Parties

Children love parties. They connect with celebrations and rituals. You can have birthday parties for composers as part of group class, or you can encourage students to celebrate their favorite composers with their families at home. Celebrations can include listening to the composer's works, learning about his life, or playing his works. Birthday decorations and snacks add to the fun.

January

Mozart – January 27, 1756

Schubert – January 31, 1797

Scriabin – January 6, 1871

February

Chopin – February 22, 1810

Handel – February 23, 1685

Mendelssohn – February 3, 1809

March

J.S. Bach – March 21, 1685

Bartok – March 25, 1881

Haydn – March 31, 1732

Ravel – March 7, 1875

Rimsay-Korsakov – March 18, 1844

Vivaldi – March 4, 1678

Wolf – March 13, 1860

April

Prokofiev – April 27, 1891

Rachmaninoff – April 1, 1873

May

Brahms – May 7, 1833

Fauré – May 12, 1845

Tchaikovsky – May 7, 1840

Wagner – May 22, 1813

June

Schumann – June 8, 1810

R. Strauss – June 11, 1882

Stravinsky – June 17, 1882

July

Mahler – July 7, 1860

August

Debussy – August 22, 1862

September

Dvořák – September 8, 1841

Gershwin – September 26, 1898

Schoenberg – September 13, 1874

October

Ives – October 20, 1874

Liszt – October 22, 1811

Saint-Saëns – October 9, 1835

Verdi – October 10, 1813

November

Copland – November 14, 1900

Hindemith – November 16, 1895

Joplin – November 24, 1868

December

Beethoven – December 16, 1770

Berlioz – December 11, 1803

Franck – December 10, 1822

Puccini – December 22, 1858

Note: This is not intended to be an extended list of composers. Feel free to add your own personal favorites. With notable exceptions, the list focuses on composers for the piano.

Students' Birthdays

A child's birthday is one of the most significant days of the year. Most teachers remember their students' birthday with cards, certificates, or small gifts. We can augment that experience by helping students discover their "birthday buddies" – the composers who have the nearest birthday dates to theirs. Students can celebrate their birthday months with two musical activities:

1. Students can play a work by their birthday buddy composer.

2. Students can arrange their own version of "Happy Birthday to You," inserting the composer's name. They can play it in different styles and create a medley.

3. Students can play the role of their composer and be "interviewed" about his or her life and works by a parent or another student.

December group class can celebrate Beethoven's birthday buddies; January group class can celebrate Mozart's birthday buddies; May group class can celebrate Brahms' birthday buddies, etc.

Educational Music Videos

Numerous excellent music education video series are available. Music videos can be shown as part of group class. If it is necessary to divide students into groups by age, younger children can view a video while the older group is covering advanced material. Older students can view a video while younger children are involved in music games. Performing for one another should always be an inclusive, shared experience.

Due to a shortage of time, you may not want to use group class time to view videos. In that case, you may want to create a lending library, so students can check out videos for home viewing, based on the theme of the month.

Contact music catalog companies (listed at the end of this chapter) to purchase videos or explore the offerings at your local library or video store. Some of my personal favorites are as follows:

For young children:
Carnival of the Animals – Magical Musical Trip to the Zoo
Peter and the Wolf
Wildlife Symphony

For intermediate/advanced students:
The Joy of Bach – Series also includes (Vision Video):
Handel, Noble Prince of Music
Mozart, the Man and his Music

Composers' Special Video Series includes (Hal Leonard Corp.):
Handel's Last Chance
Beethoven Lives Upstairs
Bach's Fight for Freedom
Bizet's Dream
Liszt's Rhapsody
Strauss, The King of 3/4 Time
Rossini's Ghost

Wynton Marsalis on Music Series (Sony Productions):
Listening for Clues
Tackling the Monster
Why Toes Tape
Sousa to Satchmo

Piano Grand – a Smithsonian celebration (PBS)
Leonard Bernstein's Young People's Concerts
The Cliburn – Playing on the Edge (Peter Rosen Productions, Van Cliburn Foundation)

Integrating Books, Storytelling, and Imagery

Imagination is the playground of the young child's mind. When channeled creatively, the imagination can become the child's best teacher. Creating stories and using books are effective ways to introduce new musical pieces during the private lesson and to celebrate learned pieces at group class.

Teachers and students together can create a story based on the song. The student may write a poem or lyrics for the song or present it in picture book form complete with illustrations.

Let's use the Suzuki *Book 1* literature as examples. One student and his mother created a fun story for "Long, Long Ago" about a battle between a giant and a small man. When the giant finally ate the man, the giant had a tummy ache. The lyrics began, "Long, long ago in a land far away, there lived a giant, there lived a man." "Little Playmates" can be a day in the park. "Good-bye to Winter" is a journey through the seasons. "Chant Arabe" is an adventure by camel through the hot dusty desert. "Eccosaise" can be the yodelers echoing back and forth after a day of mountain climbing.

Frank Asch's *Starbaby* and Emilie Boon's *Peterkin Meets a Star* are excellent books for introducing the "Twinkle Variations." In Boon's book, Peterkin makes friends with a star and takes him home. When the star becomes ill, Peterkin realizes that he must put the star back in the sky. When he does, the star recovers and is happy again. This story offers a wonderful opportunity to play the "Twinkles" in major and minor keys.

Numerous books based on folks songs are available. They are illustrated versions of the lyrics; the music and lyrics are usually included in the back of the book. We understand from Orff, Kodály, and Suzuki that familiar folk songs from our culture are the best literature for beginning musicians.

Pick your favorite folk song – "Down by the Bay", "Mama Don't Allow", "The Wheels on the Bus", "Old MacDonald", "Hush Little Baby", "She'll Be Comin' 'Round the Mountain", "The Old Lady who Swallowed a Fly", "Itsby Bitsy Spider", "Down by the Station", "Farmer in the Dell", "Hush Little Baby", "Miss Mary Mack", "Yankee Doodle". These and many more are available in book form. Relevant to the Suzuki literature, several versions of "Aunt Rhody", "Mary Had a Little Lamb", and "London Bridge" exist.

The use of imagination and books motivates the Suzuki teacher as well as the Suzuki student. No longer are we teaching the same piece over and over. It is a different adventure with each student. The student feels that his or her interpretation is the "special one." Characters and events in the stories can be fun tools for reminding children about dynamics, contrasts, themes, and more.

Any high quality children's book, not limited to music books, can play a role in inspiring a child's interest in a song. For example, *Chester's Way* by Kenvin Henkes is a wonderful tale about making friends and can accompany "Little Playmates." *The Twelve Dancing Princesses* provides a magical backdrop for learning the *Book 2* minuets. A favorite Christmas story can accompany "Christmas Day Secrets."

Book orchestrations are powerful ways to engage a group of young students in the music making process. While the book is read aloud, students create (orchestrate) the sounds in the story. Songs can be composed for repetitive phrases in the book. One of my favorite book orchestrations is based on Patricia Polacco's *Thunder Cake*. Her book is filled with sounds to be created, using instruments and voices: ROAR, BAROOOOOOOOM, CRACKLE, BOOOM, KA-BANG, RUMBLE, CRASH. Chants can be composed for the countdown song, "1-2-3-4-5-6-7-8, the storm is 8 miles away" and Grandma's repetitive "I am here, child." Be on the lookout for books with potential for creating sounds and songs.

A wide variety of books about composer's lives and music history are available today, from Mike Venezia's excellent composer series to Ann Rachlin's "Famous Children Series," describing the composers' childhoods. *The Farewell Symphony* or *Pictures at an Exhibition* by A. Celenza, *Her Piano Sang: Clara Schumann* by B. Allman, *The Magic Flute* by A. Gatti, and *The Story of the Orchestra* by R. Levine are other fine examples of educational music books, often accompanied by CDs. We can provide a lending library with books as well as videos, offering folk song books, collections of songs for family sing-along fun, children's books, reference books, and catalogs for parents.

Summer Creative Arts Program

As a creative arts therapist, I have a personal bias that musicians need to experience the related arts – dance, visual arts, drama, and literature – to fully develop their own craft. The same principles of artistic expression basically govern each process and expand a view of our own art. The Matsumoto Talent Education Institute in Japan is an excellent example of an integrated program where the Suzuki philosophy is applied to the development of other skills.

Since music teachers and students probably do not have time for a supplementary program during the regular school year, the summer season may be the best time to implement an arts program when a change from routine lessons is desirable. Classes could be held daily, over a one or two week period, or once or twice a week for two months.

Ideally you can recruit other Suzuki teachers, music specialists, and arts instructors to join forces with you and provide a comprehensive program. The music component could offer experiences unavailable during the year, such as learning to play a second instrument, choral singing, improvisation/composition, or music history. A complimentary method – such as Orff, Kodály, or Dalcroze – could be incorporated.

Students should have arts exposure as well as arts experience. Not only should they be painting, drawing, weaving, sculpting, dancing, acting, making music, and writing but, in true Suzuki philosophy, be attending art museums, plays, the ballet, and concerts. If field trips are not a realistic part of the program, a list of recommended local events can be provided for students and their families.

Teachers can guide students in integrating the arts experiences. Students can paint their responses or dance to different works of music, write poetry/lyrics to their musical composition, act out scenes inspired by great paintings, and more. The goal of the creative arts program is to fully experience the whole artistic process. The creative possibilities are endless. An extended summer program could culminate in a performed "opera" with students' poems set to their composed music, dancing, acting, sets painted, costumes designed, etc. – all products of the children's experiences.

Let's end this section with two reality checks:

1. To develop a summer arts program, you need not be expert in every area of music education and the related arts. You need to enlist other specialists to help. Hopefully these teachers will invite their students to attend and experience the music component that you can offer.

2. You will not be able to offer everything in one summer session. That goal will require several years. For example, during one summer, I offered an Orff program, an art teacher taught watercolor painting and sculpture, and a dance teacher offered creative movement classes. The next summer, a Kodály teacher focused on sol-feg and choral skills while a different dance teacher taught the students dances throughout the history of music. Students knew how to play waltzes, minuets, and allemandes but didn't understand that people had actually danced to the music. They were not only exposed to a different period of music each week, but they also learned the corresponding dance forms.

If you do not have access to a dance instructor, you may be interested in the video series, *How to Dance Through Time* (Dancetime Publications, Kentfield, CA). One of the videos focuses on Baroque social dance.

The Annual "Recital"

What was your best recital experience? What was your worst recital experience? Were you a natural performer who loved the spotlight, or were you a fearful musician who dreaded the stress of performance? Did you enjoy solo performing or playing in ensembles? Musicians perform in a variety of settings. Our students need these options as well.

The greatest stress I experienced while performing in countless recitals was a fear that I would forget my memorized piece. When I was ten years old, I forgot my recital piece four measures from the end! I could not remember how to end the song. I began improvising, and the piece seemed to go on forever. I finally ended it and was horrified at my memory loss. These performance memories can remain with us for a lifetime.

Our job as teachers is to try our best to eliminate those negative experiences. Success breeds success; perceived failure breeds failure. Most students dread performance. Realizing that fear and stress cause the brain to downshift and freeze, it makes perfect sense that our students will not perform well under typical recital conditions. That is why a student can play a well-prepared piece flawlessly during the lesson before the recital and then make new mistakes or fall apart during performance.

My question became, "Why continue this torturous tradition? What is the purpose of the annual end-of-the-year recital?" I concluded that performance can be a positive, worthwhile experience when individually tailored for the student.

Performing is a learned skill that improves with practice. Students work hard and should celebrate sharing their music and progress with their peers. But it should be a celebration of learning and not a dreaded event. It should be primarily for the students, not for the audience. Families and friends are certainly welcome but they are not the focus. The first thing I did was eliminate the word "recital", with all its associations, and replace it with "piano party." The final piano party became the culmination of the group class program.

Piano parties should be fun. If students are not looking forward to these events, then something is wrong. Since the piano party is their celebration, students should participate in planning it. In addition to solo performances, duets, two piano works, ensemble playing, and works improvised and composed by students should be included.

Our favorite activity is to create a musical journey in which students write the script, linking all the performed works together. This is the ultimate cooperative learning experience. Each student is responsible for writing the bridge before playing his or her piece and reading it. You can imagine the hysterical stories that have been created, with "Aunt Rhody" traveling by boat ("Lightly Row") to marry the "Happy Farmer." Students are encouraged to come in costume with props and be as dramatic as they desire. One year my students created a "Time Travel" script, with the Ghost of Piano Past, Piano Present, and Piano Future visiting a student who hated to practice.

My favorite Christmas piano party rendition was one student's medley of "Batman" and "God Rest Ye Merry, Gentlemen." He called it, "Batman comes to Bethlehem." "God Rest Ye Merry, Gentlemen" with the accompanying "Batman" bass was especially effective, and my other students wanted to know where they could buy the arrangement.

The last group class preceding the final piano party is the dress rehearsal, which is probably more fun than the planned event. Instead of dreading performing for strangers, students are excited to share their musical story with their families. No party is complete without refreshments; students and families enjoy the feasting that follows.

Awards are an equally important part of the final piano party. These are not practice record or performance awards; there are no winners or losers, or even first, second, or third place awards. These awards are as individual as the students. Each honor is bestowed for unique progress made during the year. Every student is "best" at something, no matter how unusual the skill may seem. Like any awards ceremony, I describe the prize-winning skill first and then announce the recipient's name. The other students enjoy trying to guess who is the next award recipient. They have come to appreciate each other's strengths. Each student receives a certificate or trophy, a gift certificate for ice cream or a movie, or some other fun trinket. A grab bag is a fun activity for Christmas group class.

An equally fun celebration following the annual piano party is to have a summer group class to view the video of the spring performance. Students should also be encouraged to give "solo recitals" in their homes for family and friends. Suzuki book parties, where students celebrate the completion of the book by playing their favorite pieces, can be an informal yet fun way to honor their accomplishment. Some families have a tradition of celebrating Suzuki Book 1 completion with hot fudge sundaes, *Book 2* with pizza, etc.

Suzuki book recitals can be as unique and meaningful as the families involved. Last year two of my students, a brother and sister, missed our Christmas group class due to illness. They had planned to play pieces from their upcoming joint *Book I* party, which was also cancelled due to a family emergency. Their grandmother was dying. My students decided to make a videotape of their *Book I* recital and play the tape for their hospitalized grandmother on Christmas Eve. Since it was also their grandmother's birthday, they celebrated with a cake. Their mother shared with me that this was the last event their grandmother truly enjoyed before her death.

Children love parties and they love gifts. They want to present gifts of music to loved ones. They love to laugh and be silly. They long to feel unique and special. When planning music celebrations, remember to see the world through the eyes of a child.

Questions to Ponder:

Think back over your childhood recital memories. Were these positive, fun experiences or just plain terrifying?

Remember the recital experiences that you have offered your own students? What would you keep the same? What would you change?

Recommended Music Companies:

Contact these companies for a catalog. They offer an outstanding selection of books, CDs, games, videos, and MORE!

MMB Music – Creative Arts Resources

Grand Center

3526 Washington Ave.

Saint Louis, MO 63103-1019

800-543-3771

Music in Motion

PO Box 869231

Plano, TX 75086

800-445-0649

Friendship House

29355 Ranney Pkwy.

PO Box 450978

Cleveland, OH 44145

800-791-9876

General Music Store

4004 Technology Dr.

South Bend, IN 46628

800-346-4448

Music Treasures Company

PO Box 9138

Richmond, VA 23227

804-730-8800

The Music Stand (for music gifts)

2921 Peak Ave.

Longmont, CO 80504

800-717-7010

Did you know?

Brahms

Brahms and Schumann became such close friends that Schumann insisted that Brahms move into his home. Schumann suffered with mental illness and tried to commit suicide. Brahms supported Clara through that painful experience and through Schumann's death. Brahms fell in love with Clara but she never returned his love and remained devoted to Schumann and his memory.

Debussy

Debussy, a brilliant pianist and phenomenal sight-reader, was admitted to the Conservatoire at age ten. He played Chopin's F minor Concerto at age twelve. He was unfriendly towards other students and made fun of his teachers. He did not agree with Franck's instructions to modulate and called his teacher a modulating machine. His teachers were exasperated with his chord choices in his compositions.

His early marriage failed. He traveled to Russia to become the piano teacher for the children of Nadezhda von Meck, Tchaikovsky's patron, but when Debussy fell in love with the eldest daughter, he was asked to leave.

Debussy was a private man throughout life. He hated to appear in public or perform and much preferred cats to people.

Now begins the exciting process of integrating all our brainstorming ideas, learning theory principles, and music education philosophies to design your own group class program. The time has come for you to write out your plans. You will find the ideas in this chapter listed in an organized format to make it easier for you to follow.

Not only do we as teachers need to have a planned curriculum for the year, but it is helpful to provide students and their families with an annual schedule when lessons begin in the fall. Parents can then plan for the year, reserve dates on a calendar, know what material will be covered, and understand expectations for their children.

Monthly group classes can also be planned through the school year, starting in October after private lessons are established and ending with the annual spring piano party in May or June. The summer season provides a much needed break from scheduled routines and offers the opportunity for an arts program.

Your group class program will be individualized for you and your students. The main purpose of this book is to inspire you to create your own program, and the ideas listed here are meant to be a springboard but should not limit you or be thought of as an unbending structure to be copied. You are a musician and an artist, and your program should reflect your unique gifts and talents. Let your students participate in the direction of group class so it can become as creative as possible.

A general format for group class is offered here as a model, which you should adapt to your students' needs, with each class celebrating a different theme or focus while retaining similar components. The following overview is designed for an inclusive group made up of a variety of abilities and ages. Parents and siblings should be encouraged to participate in the celebration since creating a music community is a family affair. Chapter 8 will focus on the specific needs of advanced students and teenagers/adults after this chapter's focus on younger children.

Each group class should ideally include the following:

1. The Listening Assignment

Realizing that listening to high quality music is the underlying foundation of all good music education, we need to guide students in listening to a variety of music genres. A developing musician who has never heard beautiful music as a model cannot make it. Imagine studying art without seeing a painting or studying dance without attending a ballet. One cannot learn about the arts; the arts must be experienced. Music is an aural art and must be learned by listening.

Students can listen to works from a different period of music each month. The following is an example:

October – Medieval

November – Renaissance

December – Baroque

January – Classical

February – Romantic

March – 20th Century

April – Jazz

May – Name That Tune (See if students can identify works from different periods)

You will probably use a mix-and-match approach through the years, and students may listen to a specific genre from each period. One year you can focus on choral literature, another on symphonies, another on chamber music, another on concertos, etc. Explain to students that many genres are not relevant to medieval or Renaissance music.

Or you may assign a different genre each month and allow students to pick the composer. For example, try the following:

October – symphony

November – piano concerto

December – choral work

January – chamber music (with piano)

February – solo piano

March – opera or ballet

April – concerto (not piano)

May – string quartet

Perhaps a student will want to become an expert on one composer and listen to his or her works every month. This experience can help the student develop a wonderful expert report to share with the other students during the last group class.

You may also assign a different composer each month, based on the composer's birthday. For example, listen to Liszt's works in October, Beethoven's works in December, Mozart's or Schubert's works in January, Handel's or Chopin's works in February, Bach's or Haydn's works in March, and so on.

With a little creativity, you can change the theme of the listening assignments with each new year of group classes. Students can keep a journal to record their listening experiences. Just as literature students sometimes keep interactive journals to write imaginary letters to authors based on the books they are reading, music students can write letters to composers based on the works they are studying.

Students should also be attending at least one live performance a year. Nothing inspires students more than viewing an expert performing a skill that they are in the process of learning.

2. History assignment

Depending on the student's desire, this window into music history can be as involved as preparing an expert report to be shared with the class or as simple as learning two or three interesting facts about one composer. I sometimes ask, "What is the most interesting thing that you learned about this composer?" or "Tell us something new that you didn't already know." To be relevant for the student, the historical information should be based on the listening assignment or piano literature being studied. Students enjoy learning about the people who composed the music that they are listening to or playing in their daily lives.

I applaud Harold Schonberg who said that music history professors spend far too much time analyzing (sometimes over analyzing) musical works and not enough time talking about composers' lives. Composers were real people with real problems, complicated relationships, and fascinating life journeys. We understand a work much better when we understand the circumstances surrounding its creation. I highly recommend Schonberg's *The Lives of the Great Composers* as a reference book for you and your students. *Grove's Dictionary of Music and Musicians* is another excellent resource for families and is available at most public libraries. Most libraries have excellent CD collections for families who are unable to purchase recordings.

You may even try what we did one year when each student presented an arts overview of a different period of music, discussing the art, literature, dance, and theater surrounding and influencing different composers.

3. Performance

Students come to group class to share with one another what they are learning and should be invited to play one Suzuki piece and other pieces of their choice, depending on the group class theme.

4. Applied Theory Assignment – Student's Own Creation

Theory learned through method books accompanying private lessons can be shared with others at group class. Relevant assignments help students put their theoretical knowledge into practice by integrating their knowledge of keys, chords, and forms. They can transpose a piece, create a scale extravaganza, improvise on a familiar melody, create their own compositions, or even write a simple score to be performed by the other students. Students should be encouraged to compose their own creations, no matter how simple or complex.

Musical terms can be posted on the door for students to define as their password into group class.

5. Instrumental Study

Music education is our goal and is not limited to piano study. Some students will never want to play another instrument beyond the piano, but they will become better accompanists if they understand a variety of instruments. Other students will enjoy piano study as a foundation but will excel on another instrument. We can offer our students an introduction to other instruments in various ways.

For example, one year my students learned to play the recorder; another year they were introduced to the guitar. One year, different guest musicians visited group class, performing for the students and explaining how their instruments worked. Some of these musicians were students' parents and siblings, thereby reinforcing the strength of community. We focused on a different instrument group on alternate months – brass, strings, woodwinds, percussion. A voice teacher visited one group class to demonstrate how the voice was a complex and difficult instrument to master. The theme of one group class was accompanying. Students brought guest performers to this class and came prepared to accompany the instrumentalist or vocalist.

Orff activities using Orff rhythm instruments are also fun ways to introduce students of all ages to playing in an ensemble. Playing in a mini-orchestra is a rare experience for pianists, especially young ones.

6. Energizer

As an opener, closer, or needed break during class, you can use Orff activities, movement games, songs, or just plain silly party games to refocus attention and add fun to group class. Almost any game can be adapted to musical themes.

7. Snack, of course!

Families can rotate bringing a snack that is served at the end of group class.

SAMPLE PLANNING SHEET

MONTH:

PERFORMANCE THEME:

Listening assignment

History assignment

Student's Creation

Instrumental Experience

Energizer

Snack

SAMPLE YEAR PLANS

Use the following sample plans as springboards and try the mix-and-match approach.

Sample #1: Introduction to Instruments and Periods

October

Introduction to Instrument Families

Listening/History Assignment: *Peter and the Wolf*

Creation: Transpositions to minor keys

November

Introduction to Music Periods

Listening/History Assignment: Renaissance music

December

Holiday Party

Criss-Crossed Carols

Creation: Improvised medleys of Christmas carols

Listening/History Assignment: Baroque music (recommended – Christmas oratorio)

January

Introduction to String Instruments – Guest Performer

Listening/History Assignment: Classical music (recommended – symphony or string quartet)

February

Introduction to Brass Instruments – Guest Performer

Listening/History Assignment: Romantic music

March

Introduction to Percussion – Guest Performer

Orff orchestration

Listening/History Assignment: 20th century music

April

Introduction to Voice – Guest Performer

Listening/History Assignment: Choral or song literature of any period

May

Accompanying class

Listening/History Assignment: Jazz

June

Annual Piano Party

Sample #2: Birthday Themes

History Assignment: Students will complete all the listening assignments but choose one birthday composer as the focus of an expert report. They will present this to group class in the form of a TV talk show with the composer as the "guest." Students will prepare interesting questions and enlist the help of another student to act as the talk show host. The composer may even play his "latest work." The student may celebrate the composer's birthday in any fashion he or she desires.

October

Birthday Composer/Listening Assignment: Liszt

November

Birthday Composer/Listening Assignment: Copland

December

Beethoven's Birthday Party

Video: *Beethoven Lives Upstairs*

January

Birthday Composer/Listening Assignment: Mozart

February

Birthday Composer/Listening Assignment: Handel

March

Birthday Composer/Listening Assignment: J.S. Bach

Video: *The Joy of Bach*

April

Birthday Composer/Listening Assignment: Prokofieff

May

Birthday Composer/Listening Assignment: Brahms

June

Annual Piano Party

Sample #3

Instrument study for the year: introduction to recorder (during the first part of each group class)

October

Duet class

Listen to a solo piano work or duet.

November

Scale Extravaganza

Listen to a chamber work with piano.

December

Holiday duo piano works

Listen to a symphony.

January

Video: *Piano Grand – A Smithsonian Celebration*

Listen to a piano concerto.

February

Compare and contrast the lives and works of two composers from two different periods.

Listen to a choral work or opera.

March

Prepare an arts overview for a composer of your choice.

Listen to a string quartet.

April

Field trip: Attend a live concert.

May

Community service: Give a concert in a senior facility or other community center.

June

Annual Piano Party: *Chopsticks Variations* by Margo Guryan

Each student prepares 1-2 variations plus other literature of their choice.

Sample #4

Introduction to guitar during the year

October

Birthday Composer Choices: Verdi or Saint-Saens

Video: *Carnival of the Animals – Magical Musical Trip to the Zoo*

November

Birthday Composer Choices: Joplin or Hindemith

Video: Marsalis Series – *Listening for Clues*

December

Birthday Composer Choices: Berlioz, Puccini, or Franck

January

Birthday Composer Choices: Schubert or Scriabin

Video: Marsalis Series – *Tackling the Monster*

February

Birthday Composer Choices: Chopin or Mendelssohn

March

Birthday Composer Choices: Ravel, Haydn, Vivaldi, or Bartok

Video: Marsalis Series – *Why Toes Tap*

April

Birthday Composer: Rachmaninoff

Video: *The Cliburn*

May

Birthday Composer Choices: Tschaikovsky, Fauré, or Wagner

Video: Marsalis Series – *Sousa to Satchmo*

June

Birthday Composer Choices: Schumann, Strauss, or Stravinsky

Annual Piano Party: *Happy Birthday Variations* by Denes Agay

Each student plays 1-2 variations with each variation representing a different music period.

Summer Birthday Choices:

July – Mahler

August – Debussy

Sample #5 Fun 'n Games

October

Introduction to solfeg

November

Musical TV Game Show – Each student creates a version for the class based on a favorite TV game show.

December

Introduction to Jazz

Holiday Theme & Variations – Students create variations based on one Christmas theme.

January

Composer Botticelli

Students present original compositions, which may include ensemble parts for other students.

February

Book Orchestrations by Students

Listening Assignment: Listen to a favorite jazz composer.

March

Auditory Bingo

Ostinato Bass class – Students create bass patterns for other students to improvise upper parts.

April

Musical Party Game – Students adapt party games to teach musical concepts.

April Fool's class – Victor Borge gags

May

"Twister" with rhythms

"Name That Tune" based on the year's listening assignments

June

Annual Piano Party

Students present original compositions, and orchestrations with the class ensemble are encouraged.

For Beginners – Example activities to incorporate with Orff instruments:

Name symphony

Playing in the round

"Magic Music" game

"Musical Alphabet" game

"Change the Piece" game

One Final Check

When you have designed your curriculum for the year, compare it with the National Standards for Music Education to verify that your goals meet content standards. Students should be:

1. Singing alone and with others a variety of literature

2. Performing on instruments, alone and with others, a variety of literature

3. Improvising melodies, variations, and accompaniments

4. Composing and arranging music at their level

5. Reading and notating music

6. Listening, analyzing, and describing music

7. Evaluating music performances

8. Understanding the relationship of music within the spectrum of creative arts

9. Understanding music in relation to history and culture

Did you know?

Handel

Handel had a ravenous appetite. He loved to eat and enjoyed entertaining at the parties of lords and ladies. He also had quite a temper.

Keyboard duels were common practice. Handel and Scarlatti had an organ and harpsichord duel in the house of Cardinal Otoboni. They were equal as harpsichordists, but Handel was the better organist. Mozart and Clementi also once fought to a draw before the emperor of Austria.

Franck was a cocky student and transposed a required composition from C to E-flat to impress the judges at a piano competition of the Paris Conservatoire. The judges decided to award him a special prize.

> *I spent all my time playing football in high school.... I would have been horrified to be a musician, a band nerd. I thought they were in band because they had nothing better to do. But you know what? I've changed my mind. If I had to do it again, I would learn to play an instrument. I'd be in the band. I wish I had played the sax.*
>
> *Now that I have adult friends who are musicians and watch my own son, who plays trumpet in his high school band, I see how much fun they are having. Why didn't I realize this when I was in high school?*
>
> —Doug [1]

Music making is one of those unique gifts that lasts a lifetime. We can continue to enjoy making music no matter how old we are. The same can rarely be said about football, cheerleading, wrestling, or a variety of other common high school activities. These are for a season while music is for life. Music making can also be enjoyed alone or in groups. It is hard to play baseball alone as a break to relieve stress.

We focus on laying a foundation with children. We prepare them and develop their music skills for the challenges to come. When working with teens and adults, we have the exciting task of helping them to apply their skills immediately and make their music experience relevant today. Adults, especially beginners, need frequent reassurance that it is never too late to learn a new lifelong skill.

How can we accomplish this? First, think back over your own high school and young adult years and ask yourself the following:

What were your favorite high school activities?

What was your "identity?" Were you involved in music activities or were you a closet musician?

How did music affect your daily life as a teenager? Was it a chore or a joy?

My own experience began as a twelve-year-old when a teacher asked me to accompany singers and play for a graduation ceremony. As I entered high school, the opportunities multiplied. If I was not accompanying the school choirs, I was playing for the school musicals at late night rehearsals, organizing the school talent show, working for a flute teacher and accompanying her students at recitals and festivals, or playing for church services and youth choirs. While my friends were babysitting, I was earning money with numerous paid accompanying jobs.

Practicing may have been a chore, but participating in music activities with other teenagers was a joy for me. Anyone who has been involved in a high school choral or band program will tell you that these are some of the most wonderful memories of their lives. Others will tell you that their involvement in music kept them

---

[1] As qouted by newspaper columnist, Marlyn Schwartz in "76 Trombones Led the Big Parade, but did I?"

busy and away from drugs and alcohol. Music as a tool in building resiliency in young people is a hot topic today, and my own experience has endured for decades. We will cover this issue in more depth in a later chapter.

How do we as teachers provide a bridge for our advanced students to use their skills in daily life? This is relevancy defined. We give them functional skills. Our goal is to develop fluent, well-rounded pianists with a wide range of abilities. In addition to performing serious solo literature, a functional pianist is able to sight-read fluently, accompany instrumentalists and vocalists, assist choral and orchestral groups, read scores, transpose, improvise, and read lead sheets.

As a young person in high school, I once attended a dinner party honoring a young concert pianist. She was my age and was concertizing in the area. After dinner we were privileged to hear this young artist play one of her most impressive pieces. I marveled at her poise in performing and was properly intimidated. I wanted to sink into the floor, but then an interesting thing happened.

The dinner guests began to gather around the piano and wanted to sing. They assumed that this young artist could easily play for them and began putting books of music up on the piano for her. Her expression immediately turned from triumph to terror. She tried to play for them, but she could not. A vocalist wanted to perform but she could not accompany him. She could not sight-read or transpose. She had never seen a lead sheet or a choral score.

One guest asked if I would accompany the vocalist. I agreed, and the guests sang as I played for them until midnight. I thought that this incident was highly unusual until I reached college and graduate school where I was surprised to meet piano students even at the doctoral level who were deficient in functional skills. This revelation transformed my teaching focus. I realized through these experiences that pianists do not automatically learn to be functional musicians unless they are taught. This is our job.

The teenage years are when many young people choose to stop taking piano lessons, with the exception of the accomplished few. Why? This occurs when music has become irrelevant for them. One of the most significant influences in teens' lives is their friends and social world. Music will remain in their lives when it is woven into their social activities. If we do not develop our older students as functional pianists, unless they are in that top 1% of exceptional pianists who will concertize (a rare occurence), then there is no tangible reason for them to continue music study.

Do your homework in researching local opportunities and encourage your students to join a choir or band, try out for a musical, be the pianist in a youth orchestra, offer accompanying services to local instrumental and vocal teachers, accompany a local children's theater production, play for a friend's wedding, play in a jazz band, attend a music camp, accompany dance or voice classes, or participate in any number of activities. If students can start small their opportunities will mushroom.

We can help students to develop skills in preparation, but the only way to truly learn to be a functional pianist is on the job. One only learns to accompany by actually accompanying. One truly learns to sight-read when on the spot, in the pressure cooker. One must simply do it for skills to slowly improve. There is no substitute for experience.

Functional skills begin with group class activities and relevant music experiences start in the music community of fellow piano students. This is a safe place to practice functional skills without stress. Students can easily transition from Orff improvisation and ensemble playing to real world music making. Teenage students who have successfully made this transition will no longer have time to attend piano group class because they will be at a variety of rehearsals. They may need to attend bi-weekly lessons instead of weekly sessions. We as teachers then move into the role of coach or mentor. Our goal is for our students to be working, active, and independent musicians, in addition to their mastery of serious literature.

The master class format where students can discuss their progress and offer constructive suggestions is ideal for advanced students and adults. In the spirit of a cooperative community, teenage students can give back to others through community service by performing at a hospital, teaching music lessons at a day care facility, or any number of opportunities.

Be aware that there is a tremendous difference between encouraging students and pushing them. Pushing too hard can backfire because it is not in the best interest of the student. For a time while I was accompanying in a number of festivals and competitions during high school, I often had the opportunity to hear another young woman perform. She was an exceptional pianist and a true prodigy, yet it was common knowledge that her mother was living our her own dreams through her daughter. This teen received scholarships to the finest music conservatories in the country, but she turned them all down. When she graduated from high school, she left home and did not touch the piano for years. This young woman's pursuit of music was not a joy for her.

Around this same time, I began to accompany the prodigy's younger sister, who was an instrumentalist, because the mother believed that accompanying was beneath her older daughter's skills. The prodigy was a solo performer, and isolation had robbed this talented pianist of her teenage years. But it did not have to be this way. What if she had joined a jazz band or accompanied a school choir? What if she had spent fewer hours in daily practice and more time with other teenagers? What if the purpose of music making had been to enrich her life and bring her happiness? What if...?

Group Class Curriculum for Teens and Adults

Playing in Ensemble:

Duet playing with our students is one of the best ways to communicate musicality. When we as teachers play duets with them on a regular basis, we can "show them" instead of "tell them." Beginning students enjoy duet playing as much as advanced students. As part of group class, teens can follow a graduated plan and bring guest musicians to perform:

1. Play duets with their teacher.

2. Play duets with other teens.

3. Play duo piano works with other teens.

4. Accompany a vocalist.

5. Accompany instrumentalists – one brass, one strings, one woodwinds.

6. Accompany a chamber ensemble.

Such a plan can hopefully prepare students to accompany a choir or other large group.

Score Reading:

1. Students can begin choral score reading by playing hymns, with an awareness of the soprano, alto, tenor, and bass line. Each line should be played separately and in varying combinations. For example, the soprano line can be played with the bass; the tenor with the alto, etc.

2. Students can transpose hymns.

3. Students can begin playing simple choral pieces, playing the accompanying line as well as the score of choral parts.

4. Students should also try singing the different choral parts.

5. Advanced students may trying playing the following literature:

   Handel's *Messiah*

   Bach's *Magnificat*

   Brahms' *Requiem*

   Mendelssohn's *Elijah*

   Stravinsky's *Symphony of Psalms*

6. Orchestral score reading, especially learning to read alto and tenor clef, is more challenging. Helpful resources include the following:

Morris and Ferguson, *Preparatory Exercises in Score Reading.* London: Oxford University Press, 1931.

Melcher and Warch, *Music for Score Reading,* Englewood Cliffs, NJ, Prentice-Hall, 1971.

7. Advanced students may enjoy playing orchestral reductions to accompany instrumentalists who are preparing concertos.

One clef reading game has proven successful with elementary school children as well as college students. A giant staff is marked on the floor with masking tape. Students are timed as they are asked to "spell" a word with note names (eg. BAD, GAB, DAD) by standing on the staff. Young children can learn treble and bass clef notation. Professor Hansen at Columbus State University has used this game with college students to teach tenor and alto clef reading. Teams can become quite competitive.

Improvisation/Composition:

Fun group class assignments, which began as simple forms and experimentation for young students will begin to reach a more advanced level. Similar to accompanying and sight-reading, the only way to to learn to improvise is to jump in and try it.

Exposure to jazz through listening to favorite jazz composers is the foundation. Who are your favorite artists: Dave Brubeck, Claude Bolling, Duke Ellington, Miles Davis? From New Orleans jazz to fusion, encourage students to listen to a variety of styles.

A graduated sample plan follows:

1. Preparation: Students should understand the circle of fifths and be comfortable playing in a variety of keys. They should be able to play scales and all chords in every key and inversion.

2. Students can create arrangements of familiar songs by transposing major to minor and vice versa. Students should play simple pieces in at least two other keys. Beginners can easily play "Twinkle Variations" in G and A minor during the first month of lessons. One of my students was intrigued with transposing Bach's minuets – the major sections to minor and the minor middle sections to major. This can create quite a contrast.

3. Students can learn to read a lead sheet from a fake book and should be able to write their own lead sheet for their arrangements.

4. Every student should learn to play "Happy Birthday To You." I can still remember how foolish I felt when my choral teacher asked me during my first week of accompanying, "Can you play 'Happy Birthday'? It's Cindy's birthday." Without the music, I was lost. She told me that this was the one song that every pianist should be able to play, and she was absolutely right. I muddled through and immediately went home to memorize "Happy Birthday To You." Our students can learn to play this song in a variety of styles. Playing the song in a minor key is especially fun for "over the hill" parties.

5. Whether it is a Christmas piece, a familiar melody, or the student's favorite song, the student can arrange that melody in different styles (an original theme and variations): rock, boogie, blues, jazz, gospel, neo-Classical or Baroque, or any styles that the student is studying. The student will create bridges to link the songs.

6. Another fun assignment is to create a medley of different songs in the same style.

7. As students advance and become comfortable with improvising, they will naturally begin composing their own music. Whether it is a piano work or an orchestrated work for group class, advanced students should be encouraged to notate their work. We can help them "publish" their music, by photocopying and binding the pieces into a spiral book. Publishing a collection of students' compositions is fun because students can then play one another's creations.

Improvisation Sources

Over the years, I have developed my own method for teaching improvisation to students, notating chords, styles, and assignments in spiral music books. I then discovered an outstanding book for students which thoroughly covers this material and is systematic, well-organized, and attractively packaged. CDs are even included with examples by jazz combos. I highly recommend *Blues & Jazz Complete! The Most Comprehensive Source for Keyboard Players at All Levels* by Dr. Bert Konowitz, professor of music at Columbia University (Alfred Publishing). Other good resources include the following:

The Jazz Theory Book or The Jazz Piano Book by Mark Levine (Shar Music)

Jazz Hanon by Leo Alfassy (Amsco Publications)

101 Songwriting and Composing Techniques by Jack Wheaton (Alexander Publishing)

Video: *Journey Through Jazz* (Rock Roots – PBS)

The Jazz Book – From Ragtime to Fusion by Joachim Berendt, Lawrence Hill Books, NY, NY, 1989.

CD Collection: *Jazz – The Story of America's Music* by Ken Burns, Columbia/Legacy, Sony Music.

The Solo Recital

Advanced students should be comfortable performing and may enjoy preparing a solo recital. The recital should be as individual as the student. Students can begin by selecting works from the different periods of music. The creativity comes in planning the program, which can include a duet, jazz piece, personal composition, or an ensemble work with other instrumentalists. The solo recital is an ideal way for graduating seniors to celebrate the culmination of years of hard work. If they plan to continue studying music in college, this is the perfect preparation for making audition tapes and performing at the university level. If not, this is an elegant way to bring closure to a high school music career. If a solo recital is overwhelming, perhaps three or four graduating students could combine their resources to offer a joint program. For unusually accomplished and ambitious students, making a recording of their favorite works can be an exciting project. They can give these as gifts to friends and family members.

I have been amazed through the years at my adult students who have chosen to given solo programs. We call them "salon recitals," modeled after recitals given in homes during the Romantic period. These students plan every detail, from their repertoire to the desserts they serve, from the invitations to the typed program. These events are truly celebrations!

More Questions:

As an advanced pianist in high school or college, were you a well-rounded functional pianist? What were your strengths?

Think about your older, advanced students:

Are they growing as musicians or are they losing interest?

How can you help them become functional pianists?

What opportunities do their community and high school offer them?

Did you know?

Schumann did not seriously study music until he was eighteen years old. He began piano study with the renowned teacher, Friedrich Wieck. Wieck's daughter, Clara, was her father's pride and the best example of his expert teaching. Wieck was impressed with Schumann's great potential and invited him to move into their home to concentrate on his studies. All was well until Schumann and Clara fell in love and were engaged. Wieck was furious and did everything in his power to stop the marriage, but he failed.

Schumann

Liszt was famous for his ability to sight-read any piece of music, and he enjoyed playing the music of new composers. However, when Fauré sent his Ballade to Liszt, Liszt returned it, saying that it was too difficult.

Liszt

Chapter 9

At this point, I want to comfort you with a reality check. You may plan the most outstanding group class program possible and still be faced with the fact that your students have neither the time to attend the nor desire to put extra time into creative projects. Our culture moves at a breakneck speed, and most parents want their children to have every possible opportunity for growth and development. However, the dilemma is, "How do we fit it all in?" More critical, "How do we allow young people time to be children?"

Brain research has shown that daydreaming, brainstorming, playing, and spending time doing absolutely nothing are ways that children learn. The child's "work" is often perceived as a waste of time by busy adults, but structured, "productive" programs are not always in the child's best interest.

After the Great Depression, our grandparents were concerned with saving money. Our generation is consumed with saving time and sometimes our children suffer.

We as teachers are trying to plan group classes in a world of soccer practices, music lessons, baseball games, dance classes, and more. Today's young people have been called "smorgasbord kids," sampling a little bit of everything in hopes of being ideally well-rounded. Contrast this approach with the idea that young people should focus on one or two skill areas, and their discipline in striving for excellence will transfer to other areas of life.

Many programs – such as band, art, choir, and sports – were once taught within the school day. However, because of a lack of funding, these are often only available now as private or afterschool activities. Families with more than one child run in multiple directions. Each teacher and coach strives for 100% commitment, desiring their activity to be the child's top priority. Difficult choices are made at the cost of a well-rounded life. We then attempt to fit in a regular family dinner hour (which is today almost impossible), and parents end up tearing their hair out. No wonder we are all exhausted.

As teachers we need to be sensitive to the needs of our students and their families. We are required to be flexible and creative. We do not want group class to become one more stress. With this is mind, perhaps we can offer bi-monthly group classes instead of monthly group classes.

When my own children were young, I designed my group class program for their benefit. As a Suzuki teacher, I believed that if I could not share the joy of music making with my own children, then I had no business teaching other people's children. I now look back at this period in time as my "golden years." I worked with families who were unusually eager and committed to making music. Music lessons were a priority in their lives, not just one of many activities. Siblings wanted to take part in the fun. We held monthly group classes, and students went above and beyond in working on a variety of projects.

Our music community was able to bond in a unique way. My children were as excited as my students to attend class. Then these students grew up and became functional pianists. They began participating in orchestras and bands, choirs, jazz bands, musicals, and diverse musical opportunities. They moved beyond the group class experience, transitioning into the real world, which was always the goal. Just as parents need to let go as their children mature, so do teachers need to let go as students develop and their needs change.

My own children grew up to make the same transition. My oldest daughter, now pursuing the arts in college, became active in theater and dance, while continuing to accompany a youth choir. My second daughter preferred her woodwind studies to the piano and became active in different orchestras, bands, and dance programs. My younger son began studying brass instruments in addition to piano and became involved in band. I have spent my afternoons driving to endless lessons and activities just as my students' parents do. I understand their dilemma and want to support them in this life challenge. As a music community, we are all in this together.

American culture has changed, and families are running in more directions than they were a decade ago. We need a reality check. Our challenge as teachers is to provide a solid music education program in the midst of intense schedules. We will not face a more demanding task than this. In the introduction to this book, I told you that I was handing you a baton. The truth is that many of my group class ideas that worked twenty years ago are unrealistic in today's schedules. You may be currently experiencing a golden period in your own teaching years, in which you can implement a full curriculum. Or you may be challenged to adapt, carefully choosing the most important elements of a program that is tailored to your students' needs. Do not let the stresses of our culture discourage your creativity. You can still find a way to make music a joyous and fulfilling experience for your students.

Questions to Ponder:

How do you personally negotiate today's fast-paced schedule with your own family?

What challenges do your students and their families face in making time for a group class program?

What is an ideal program? What is realistic?

Did you know?

Mahler was so consumed with his music that
he ignored his wife, and she became resentful.
Mahler felt that his marriage was a failure,
and he sought help from Sigmund Freud.
Mahler was a true workaholic.

Mahler

The Suzuki music community is inclusive – not in theory but in practice – which encourages teachers to include students of all abilities and ages. No one is too old or too young to make music. Even infants benefit from music stimulation. Everyone from pre-schoolers through adults (including seniors) can learn to explore music, sing a song, or play an instrument.

The New Horizons Band, one of our four pilot programs, has successfully provided music education for seniors. These students also pursue private instruction in addition to the ensemble experience. Brain researchers agree that music education stimulates the brain and promotes lifelong learning, confirming the popular advice to: "Use it or lose it."

Students of all abilities can participate, including those with special needs as well as those with gifted abilities. We do not label individuals as disabled, implying that they are without ability. Everyone has an ability to learn, but some students may have special needs and learning differences. Dr. Levine would say that all children and adults have "special needs" depending on how their brains are uniquely wired. Today we understand that music education is not limited to note reading education. Students who are unable to read music can still enjoy making music.

The musical brain is resilient. Despite one's age or ability, every human being can have a meaningful musical experience. Even in the face of brain impairments and injuries, the ability to enjoy making music appears to remain intact.

Every exceptional child has the legal right to receive music education in public schools. Since Public Law 94-142 was passed in the 1970s, school districts have been required to provide it. Three decades later, however, in the face of funding cuts for arts programs, that mandate has not become a reality in our school systems. Music therapists are rarely hired for special education classes, and most choral and instrumental teachers feel unequipped to mainstream special needs students. Concerned parents sometimes seek out music education for their exceptional children through private music programs.

What is Music Therapy?

Shinichi Suzuki was a natural music therapist. Orff, Dalcroze, and Kodály have been equally influential in making music education available to students of all abilities. Music therapy can be defined as the treatment of disorders and problems through music. It is one of the creative arts therapies, which also include art, dance, and drama therapy. Creative arts therapists use an artistic medium to influence behavior change and are employed in hospitals, schools, and in private practice, working with a variety of populations.

Music therapy is used in clinical settings to help accident victims to regain use of their fingers through learning to play an instrument. It is also teaching individuals with respiratory or speech problems to sing. Music therapy is engaging children who struggle with reading in rhythm activities. It is using musical games and songs to encourage a child abuse victim to discuss her experience or to distract a pediatric patient from pain and alleviate the trauma of hospitalization. Music therapy is using familiar songs to prompt an aging, terminally ill patient to discuss life experiences and prepare for death. It is relieving stress through imagery and relaxation techniques. It is providing music in the delivery room to ease the birth process and to help a newborn infant discover his or her environment. Music therapy is developing group music activities to enhance self-esteem with psychiatric patients or to encourage socialization skills with developmentally disabled clients. The applications are endless. The need is identified first, and the musical experience is then tailored to meet it.

Music making provides a secure, nonthreatening environment where a relationship of trust between the therapist and client is easily established. Music making is an especially effective process because it is brain-compatible, targeting all areas of development. Clients are distracted from their limitations, and disorders are more easily treated.

Music therapy is a profession, requiring specialized degree training and board certification, but the process has applications for all of us. Committed to celebrating music making skills in any individual, regardless of age or ability, Suzuki would surely have viewed music education for students with special needs as an extension of music therapy.

In light of the attack on our country on September 11, 2001, let us remember that Suzuki developed his method in response to the devastating effects of World War II on Japanese children. Suzuki was concerned for the whole child and for a child's emotional, physical, and mental well-being apart from any musical product. Similar to music therapists, Suzuki believed that music capabilities will transfer to other areas of life. His goal was the full development of the human potential and an enriched, happier life.

Suzuki believed that music brought healing to hurting children. He refused to accept that any human being was a failure. His success with special needs children was based on patience and persistence. He taught by moving at a slower pace, requiring more repetitions and breaking tasks down into the smallest parts possible. He believed that one success breeds another. He saw physical limitations improve as a result of studying music. Suzuki created a positive, loving, and safe environment for the child, parent, teacher, and music community.

At Juilliard, kids are hypercritical of each other and very competitive. The teachers expect, and in most cases get, technical perfection. But this wasn't about that. The soldiers didn't care that I had so many memory slips I lost count. They didn't care that when I forgot how the second movement of the Tchaikovsky went, I had to come up with my own insipid improvisation until I somehow got to a cadence. I've never seen a more appreciative audience, and I've never understood so fully what it means to communicate music to other people.

—William Harvey, a violinist studying at the Juilliard School of Music, after playing for rescue workers in New York City following the September 11 attack

Did you know?

All of J.S. Bach's sons became musicians. Several of his boys died young, and one was developmentally disabled. But it was not C.P.E Bach or J.C. Bach who were their father's pride. Bach's favorite son was Wilhelm Friedemann, an exceptionally talented young man, who was also a wanderer, a drunkard, and emotionally ill-adjusted.

C.P.E. Bach

Both Haydn and Mozart were short in stature and their faces were pitted from smallpox, which was common in that day. Haydn was a secure, well-adjusted man, yet he did not have a happy childhood. He once said that he received more beatings than food. His father was a wagon maker, and many of Haydn's skills were self-taught. When he worked in the service of the Esterhazy family, Haydn saw his position as a servant and ate with the help.

Haydn

> *Resiliency is often the result of one person or one opportunity or one caring family member, teacher, or friend who encouraged a child's success and welcomed his or her participation.*
>
> —Bonnie Benard

Resiliency can be defined as the ability to bounce back after experiencing adversity, risk, or stress. Resilient materials return to their original state without rupturing after a period of compressed stress. Resilient people bounce back after enduring adversity that would harm other people. Educators and psychologists have been asking why some people recover while others do not survive abuse, neglect, poverty, chronic illness, alcoholic or mentally ill parents, the death of a family member, or other stressful life experiences. Why do a majority of children become healthy, competent adults while others are unable to break a negative cycle?

Bonnie Benard, a pioneer in the study of resiliency, developed a strengths-based approach, encouraging us to look at the positive factors in resilient people instead of focusing on the negative risk factors. The first question she suggests asking is "What is right with you?" She suggests emphasizing childrens' strengths not their limitations. In an effort to help children, many programs have been developed for children "at risk." Resiliency advocates agree that fostering resilience is a process not a program, and developing healthy, supportive relationships is the foundation. The stigma of the "at risk" label does more harm than good. Just as it is better to focus on students' abilities (vs. their disabilities), we can focus on children's strengths and their resources for overcoming adversity. The theme of resiliency work is communicating to children that what is right with them is more important than what is wrong with them. This is the "resiliency attitude", and hopefulness is a key component.

Protective Factors

Benard also found that resilient people are socially competent in a caring community, know how to problem solve, have a sense of purpose and hope for the future, are independent, self-disciplined, and have a healthy sense of self-esteem. She identifies three categories of protective factors, which help kids living with adversity to not only survive, but also to thrive:

1. Caring and support

2. Positive expectations

3. Active participation

Resilient children experience a positive, nurturing relationship with parents, extended family members, or mentoring adults. They experience a caring and safe community. They are equipped with skills for the future and have a sense of purpose with hope for the future. Benard's studies show that mentor-rich environments, in which adults genuinely care for students and have high yet realistic expectations, are the most effective. Cooperative learning communities are ideal settings to nurture resiliency.

Today resiliency is not viewed as a program for children at risk but as coping skills that should be nurtured in all children. In reviewing the resiliency literature, I have found recommendations quite similar to the crisis intervention tools I learned as a music therapist. Every human being experiences adversity, stress, and risk in life.

Dr. Peter Benson lists 40 assets that protect young people against a wide range of risk behaviors. He moves from generalities (e.g., expectations, esteem, support, etc.) to specific recommendations, focusing on health and prevention. One asset involves spending three or more hours per week participating in creative activities – lessons or practice in music, theater, dance, or art. Arts experiences provide a constructive use of time, which builds lifelong skills and esteem. A recent survey completed by the "What's Your Anti-Drug Campaign?" found music to be the number one anti-drug choice among 85,000 students.

Researchers on resiliency agree that developing a special talent or hobby that promotes self-esteem is often the key factor in developing resilient young people. Competence breeds confidence. Music teachers can be assured that they play a significant role in helping young people to be resilient. In light of designing school or private music programs, the following applies:

1. Caring and support = nurturing and supportive music teachers/mentors

2. Positive expectations = music skills for a purpose today and hope for the future

3. Active participation = involvement in a caring and supportive music community

In my high school music program there was a girl who had been sexually molested by her father. Another young man had an alcoholic mother. Another had a severely disabled brother and was understandably neglected by his parents. Another young man came from a home filled with violent arguments between his parents. Sometimes this boy would sleep outside my house in his car because it was safer than going home. I knew these kids and others with similar life situations, from our music program. They often visited my home on the weekends to sing around the piano, play other instruments, laugh, and eat, safe from alcohol and drugs. Lest you assume that this is a dated phenomenon, my own children have experienced a similar safe community in their current music programs.

When my husband was thirteen years old, his father and brother died in an accident, and he credits his high school band with being the "family" who helped him survive that tragedy. The role of the arts in resiliency and helping at risk-kids may be a current driving force in education, but the concept is not new. What is new is that teachers and therapists are recognizing at-risk behaviors and identifying the influences and factors that may protect children from permanent damage. Hopefully children are no longer falling between the cracks of educational systems.

Community membership and peer acceptance are critical to teens. We as teachers can equip teens to participate in a productive community. Kids with problems have often found a safe haven in music programs. The skills, mentoring, and comfort they receive from learning to make music is often their only anchor through a chaotic adolescence. In sharing the gift of music, you can make a tremendous difference in the lives of young people.

Developing resiliency is first and foremost a person-to-person process.
Resiliency is forged in the crucible of caring human relationships.

—Nan Henderson

Questions to Ponder:

Did you personally benefit from a high school music program? Did you rub shoulders with kids who today would be considered at risk?

Do you have students who need a caring mentor? Can you volunteer your services as a music teacher/mentor through a community organization?

Though you may not have students who are at risk or have diagnosed disorders, are you aware of the changes or traumas in your students' lives (such as divorce, a death in the family, a personal crisis)? Do you see yourself as one of the support systems in your students' lives?

Did you know?

Brahms

Brahms began playing the piano in public at age ten. He played in waterfront bars and bordellos to bring money into his family. This early experience scarred him, and he confined his sexual encounters to prostitutes during his life.

Mozart

Mozart was the most exploited prodigy in the history of music. Despite his musical fame, he remained a child in his personal life and was unable to function as a capable adult. His father emotionally crippled him, and Mozart spent his life trying to escape his father's domination and constant criticism. His father could only point out the weaknesses in Mozart's life, and they suffered a classic love/hate relationship. Mozart never married, and he found relationships to be difficult. He died penniless.

Beethoven

Beethoven had a similar relationship with his father, who was a dissatisfied court musician. Beethoven's father hoped that Beethoven would become another Mozart. Yet Beethoven rebelled against his father and every form of authority. Teachers found him difficult to work with because Beethoven insisted on breaking all the rules.

When Beethoven's brother died, he fought a custody battle to take his nephew away from the boy's mother and won. Beethoven made his nephew's life miserable, and the boy tried to commit suicide. He told police that Beethoven tormented him.

Chapter 12

Teaching Music Students with Special Needs

> *If a hundred meter race is carried out by several children, there are some who are faster than others. But even those who are slow will reach the goal if they continue to run.*
>
> —Dr. Masaaki Honda

Music teachers with special needs students agree that there is no magic formula or set of definitive techniques that insures success. The approach is as individual as the student, depending on his or her needs and abilities (strengths and weaknesses). Yet three keys to success remain constant:

1. Most important is the relationship between the student and teacher/therapist. A caring relationship of trust built between them is the best motivator for learning when set in a safe and nonthreatening environment.

2. Tasks must be broken down into the smallest parts possible to achieve success. Teachers should patiently move at a slow pace, requiring numerous repetitions. The student should be presented with small, attainable goals on a regular basis. This is termed task analysis. With perseverance on both the teacher's and student's parts, students will celebrate their accomplishments.

3. Labels are prohibited. Ability development is the theme, and strengths are the focus. We view our students (not "diagnosed clients" or "at risk students") as capable young people who can meet our expectations. The expectations can be high yet realistic for the individual.

Just as a picture is worth a thousand words, so is a tangible illustration worth numerous theoretical instructions. In the following examples, parents and students have generously offered to share their experiences, showing us how music has changed their lives. In this chapter, you will read about students of all ages, from pre-school through adult, each with a uniquely wired brain. Some students have diagnosed disorders, while others have been labeled as children at risk. I have included notes when relevant. View these stories as real-life summaries of the concepts discussed in the previous chapters.

Young Students

Our son has a speech impediment. Today, at eight years of age, he is doing well but it has been a challenging road. At two years of age, he had the speech skills of a one year old. When he reached the age to attend kindergarten, he could not say his name. We decided not to place him in a traditional classroom but to home school him with the support services of speech therapists and reading specialists. Reading was a struggle because sound/letter matching was affected by his speech. For example, because he pronounced "dis" instead of "this," he did not understand why the word was written with "th."

The cause of my son's speech problems is a mystery. He had a choking accident and was deprived of oxygen when he was one year old. Years later, he fell from a tree, cracked his skull, and was in ICU for a week. We can only speculate if these traumas may have affected his speech development.

My son has always loved music. Whenever he has access to a piano, he plays – not bangs as most young children do – but actually plays with sensitivity. Our pediatrician suggested that we consider giving him piano lessons. He told my son that some of the most famous musicians had speech and hearing problems. He felt this was a way that our son could communicate.

Making music became our son's passion. Playing the piano gave him a sense of success and accomplishment, a skill he could enjoy apart from his struggles with speech. This young boy's reading has improved, and rhythm activities are known to help with reading skills. He not only loves to make music but wants to share it with others. When we visited a convalescent hospital for a Christmas sing-along, he asked to play "Jingle Bells" for the residents. He loves to sing and enjoys participating in church choir musicals.

Note: The pediatrician mentioned gave this child the "resiliency attitude" when he encouraged him to study music and explained that famous musicians had similar struggles. This young boy's music making transferred to other areas of of life, sharing music in the community and participating in a church choir. Rhythm skills are key foundation blocks of learning to read.

*   *   *

My daughter is an intelligent ten-year-old with perceptual motor difficulties. Experiencing a severe allergic reaction to a virus when Lisa was a toddler, her immune system attacked her myelin sheath, causing cerebral ataxia. Lisa loves literature, but the actual decoding of the words is difficult for her. She enjoys making music, but note reading is a barrier to achievement. Because she is bright, Lisa is aware of her limitations, causing her frustration and a sense of failure. I home school Lisa to protect her from the stigma that special classes would bring.

Observing that Lisa enjoyed music and dancing, we placed her in Suzuki music lessons and ballet classes. We have observed a marked improvement in Lisa's motor skills. Her small motor coordination is slowly improving. The Suzuki Method focuses on Lisa's auditory strengths. She experiences success, regardless of her struggle with note reading. We use a color coding system to help her learn to read music.

Lisa works hard and enjoys making music. Music invites her to risk being in new situations, such as group classes and recitals, instead of simply observing life as a fearful outsider. She does not need to fear failure. Music lessons and dance have been bridges, connecting her to a normal childhood.

Note: Color coding notes is a common practice with children who struggle with visual discrimination. Each music note is literally marked with a distinct color. Some students create their own individual approach (e.g., C=red, D=blue, E=yellow). Rainbow solfege is an actual system used in classrooms, reinforcing the learning of notes with specific matching colors. Many students with visual learning differences have discovered this approach on their own and "colored" their music, much to the dismay of traditional music teachers. Did you know that Isaac Newton assigned colors to the tones of the major scale in the 1700s? Did you know that both Scriabin and Messiaen had synesthesia, experiencing colors with their music?

Working with students who struggle with visual discrimination is different than working with visually impaired or blind students. Blind students will find quick success with the Suzuki Method. When ready, they can be introduced to Braille music reading. Resources are listed in the bibliography.

*   *   *

Nicole was born with a neuro-muscular condition, similar to cerebral palsy. We noticed that she was developing at a slower rate than her older siblings, and we began intervention when she was two years old. She has grown up with the support services of home teachers, special school classes, physical therapists, speech therapists, and occupational therapists.

Nicole has very poor muscle tone and experiences difficulty with her balance. She struggles with processing physical tasks and has poor visual discrimination. Reading symbols, especially mathematical symbols, is difficult. When she is discouraged or faced with challenging physical and visual tasks, Nicole tends to give up quickly.

Our entire family enjoys music, and Nicole is no exception. She loves to sing and listen to all types of music. We decided to pursue music lessons because she often played familiar songs on the piano or composed her own tunes.

Nicole's muscle tone has improved with piano study. She is strengthening the muscles in her hands and arms through using them to make music. When she is playing the piano, she is completely focused. She loves to practice and does not give up when tasks become difficult, which she does in other therapy sessions. She is learning to read music and perseveres to learn the new symbols. We attribute this concentration to her desire to make music. She is highly motivated to play the piano. Physical and visual tasks that are grueling in occupational therapy sessions are fun during music lessons. Music training has given her a new confidence and enhanced self-esteem.

Note: Music making worked on developing skills similar to Nicole's other therapy sessions. Yet Nicole saw music as an immediate reward for her hard work, which motivated her to persevere, thereby improving other developmental areas.

* * *

My son was miserable in school. Because of his intense emotions and deep sensitivity, he was continually a target for bullies. He stopped wanting to learn, struggled with depression, and told us that he didn't want to live. His teacher was not understanding or tolerant. Physicians were unsure about prescribing medication. We decided to home school our son and give him a chance to recover.

We included piano lessons in his home school curriculum. The music served as an outlet for his bottled up emotions. He started to enjoy learning again and wanted to succeed. As he mastered the piano, his confidence and self-esteem grew. Making music seemed to calm him and give him a safe place to release his intense feelings. Playing the piano helped him focus on a specific task. I can see that he is developing a lifetime skill, which will provide an anchor in the future.

Note: Feeling powerless and hopeless, this student had lost his desire to live. Music making was one way that he began to take back control of his life by feeling confident about his progress and enjoying a safe place to release his emotions.

* * *

In my son's classroom hangs a poster that states:

A successful learner...

- has a positive attitude.

- understands and accepts responsibility.

- listens attentively.

- is able to focus.

- respects and works effectively with others.

- is organized.

- takes risks.

- is reflective.

My ten-year-old son does not possess many of these attributes associated with successful learning. He has attention deficit disorder, the inattentive type. Because my son is mellow and not hyperactive, his serious learning disabilities are not obvious. Yet the gap between his intellect and school work is glaring. He is painfully aware that his classmates stay focused, work more efficiently, and learn faster than he does.

My son does stay focused when learning music. He has studied the piano for four years and the trumpet for one year. He became involved in his school band program. Playing the piano and exploring different sounds calms him. He enjoys making music, even though he struggles with differentiating between lines and spaces when trying to read music. His pride in completing a piece reinforces his self-esteem, countering the painful experiences in school.

Another important benefit of music lessons is the one on one attention my son receives from a teacher, his own personal cheerleader for success. Her willingness to tailor the lessons according to my son's unique learning style, her sense of humor, and her patience have been an ideal fit for him. At age five, my son was intrigued with goggles. At his insistence, he and his first music teacher both wore swimming goggles during one entire music lesson.

My older son also has learning difficulties and battles depression. He studied piano and guitar as a child and continues to play as an adult. Making music has been his method for bringing balance to his life and working out his emotional inner struggles.

Note: Children who have trouble focusing on academic tasks at school can successfully focus on music tasks. This experience builds their confidence as they learn to transfer these skills to other areas. This child was successful in private music lessons, which transferred to success in the band program at school, providing him with a link to success in the classroom.

Teens

My son, Steven, was in the intensive care unit of Children's Hospital for his first six months of life. He was born 14 weeks premature and weighed 2 pounds, 11 ounces. Being on a respirator for five months caused speech delays and fluency problems. Steven also had a severe intercranial bleed following his birth, which caused reading comprehension problems later in life.

Steven was placed in a special education class in elementary school due to his motor and speech delays. He was mainstreamed during high school with the support of district therapists.

Steven seemed to have a good ear for music. We noticed that he played pieces on the piano by ear and wanted him to have music lessons as a young teen. Today Steven is 19 years old, and the benefits of music training have been remarkable. Most important, Steven's self-esteem has visibly increased. He does not like to talk in front of people, but he does not hesitate to play the piano for them. Steven is able to focus on a musical task, master it, and enjoy a great sense of achievement. He communicates through his music.

Music is one way that Steven can express himself and cope with the emotional challenges of adolescence. It is difficult for any teenager to verbalize feelings but especially difficult for those with speech problems. This coping method was critical when Steven's grandfather died. Steven was very close to his grandparents, and this was a difficult time for our family. Steven coped with his loss by trying to support his grandmother in her grief.

We found a favorite piece of music that Steven's grandmother had played when she was young. Steven worked very hard to master this challenging piece. Practicing this piece helped him release his grief and raw emotions. The more he played, the more he experienced healing. When he finally performed this piece for his grandmother, the smile on his face reflected his accomplishment and healing. He will always treasure the embrace that followed his performance, knowing that he brought a moment of happiness to his grieving grandmother.

Six months later, Steven's grandmother's health had deteriorated and she lay dying. While she was in ICU, Steven went to his music teacher's house to record a tape of his grandmother's favorite songs. Although he could not visit her, he could touch her through his music. Again this project helped my son to deal with his own continuing grief. Steven's tape was played at his grandmother's bedside during her final days.

Through the years, music became Steven's intimate language, and it reached places in us where words have failed.

Note: Learning to make music not only helped Steven to focus, accomplish goals, communicate effectively, and feel pride in his achievements, but it also gave him the tools to cope during the crises of his life.

Terminal Illness

I knew grief early in life. My father, an excellent musician, died when I was seven years old. The music in our home left with him. I longed to pass that gift of music on to my own children someday.

Then my husband and I had a beautiful baby girl, who had the terminal illness, cystic fibrosis. There was no cure. We couldn't imagine how our sick child would have any sort of happiness in her shortened life. We filled her life with music, listening to a variety of recordings. She began to sing, beat on everything in sight with incredible rhythm, and pick out familiar melodies on her small keyboard. She began studying the piano at age five. Some of her musical compositions won awards in elementary school.

She became involved in the school band program in fifth grade. She could not play a wind instrument because she lacked the respiratory capacity, but she could play the drums. She turned out to be an outstanding percussionist and received a professional drum set from the Make-A-Wish foundation. She began taking private drum lessons in addition to piano study.

She is now a percussionist in her high school jazz band, marching band, symphonic band, and drum line. No matter how ill she feels, she says, "I have to go to school today. The band needs me." She is part of a team. This purpose is what keeps her going and gives her hope about the future. Music has given her a confidence and purpose that most seriously ill children do not experience. She has a community of supportive, caring friends in the band. She has hopes and dreams for tomorrow, and this vision is critical to her daily well-being.

Note: Having a sense of purpose and vision for the future is critical for terminally and chronically ill children. They must live to the fullest the days that they have left. One of my friend's daughters was learning to read while she was dying of leukemia and needed a pair of glasses. The callous optometrist said, "Don't waste your money on glasses. She's going to die soon anyway" Making music has been and will continue to be the joyous lifeline for many ill children and their families.

Impact on a Family

The question I am asked most frequently is, "How did your family get started in music?" It all began when I felt that my quiet middle child needed something special all her own, an outlet for her individuality to bloom. I had observed that she learned in different ways from my other children. I was frustrated that we were not on the same wavelength. Yet I did not want to have her diagnosed or labeled. My daughter needed to learn in creative ways, and music ended up being the key to her flourishing development.

Our music teacher appreciated the special qualities in my daughter that I had struggled to understand. I saw my daughter through new eyes, embracing the unique beauty in her artistic personality. Our mother-daughter-teacher triangle expanded into a music community. My other children were exposed to making music through attending my daughter's group classes. Soon all my seven children were taking piano or violin lessons and participating in a variety of music activities.

Music touched my daughter's heart and gave her a language to express herself. Piano has continued to be her primary instrument, but she also plays the violin, cello, and harp. She taught herself to play the guitar and dulcimer. She performs in two community orchestras and teaches beginning piano lessons to several students, including her younger siblings.

My daughter has shared with me that she sits at the piano and plays her heart out when she is upset. She has found music to be healing when she is suffering. She plans to major in music education and become a music teacher.

Today we have seven children who enjoy making music. Calling themselves the Wellspring Fiddlers, they play a variety of instruments and perform for various celebrations and functions. At each performance, without fail, someone approaches me to ask, "How did your family get started in music?" That musical experience changed our lives.

A Musical Miracle

Today my son is a music major in college, specializing in vocal performance. He plans to become a music teacher or enter the music ministry. This accomplishment is a miracle because my son only knew failure in school when he was a child.

I knew that our son, Jeff, was not ready to enter kindergarten as his sister had been. He didn't like to cut with scissors, draw, and seldom tried to write. No matter how we tried to encourage him with a variety of activities, his small motor coordination did not improve. Twenty five years ago, teachers generally did not understand learning differences. Jeff was miserable at school. Even though he was intelligent, administrators wanted to place him in a special day class because he could not write or spell. We were trapped in a maze, and no one seemed to be able to help us.

Homework that took other students 30 minutes would require two hours of Jeff's time. The sense of failure and frustration was building. Our gentle child was now pushing and shoving his classmates and was daily falling farther behind in school. We could see that we were losing him, and we as parents felt like failures too. We feared that Jeff would go down that well traveled path of rebellion, anger, drugs, and alcohol in response to his low self-esteem. Targeting kids at risk and resiliency were unheard of topics.

After years of messages of failure and "you just need to try harder," Jeff was finally diagnosed with learning disabilities. We then applied for a pilot home study program. The mentor teacher was a godsend. She understood learning disabilities because she had personally struggled with dyslexia. In addition to using different educational methods, she said that it was critical to rebuild Jeff's self-concept and rekindle his love for learning. Our mission was to find an activity in which he could succeed and find enjoyment. Being a creative child, Jeff began having piano lessons with a local music therapist. We had no idea how this experience would change our lives.

Jeff had an excellent ear and learned rhythms quickly. He had auditory strengths that had not been tapped. The Suzuki Method used by our teacher allowed for immediate success. The therapist wisely stayed away from note reading. Jeff diligently practiced and looked forward to each lesson. Soon he began creating his own compositions and proudly shared them with his teacher and others. This music program became a safe haven for Jeff, a place of achievement and success. His teacher corrected mistakes with positive modeling, never saying "No!" My son had heard those words enough to last a lifetime.

Music was visibly healing Jeff's wounds. My mother noticed, "We're starting to get our happy little boy back." Jeff was blossoming in his music studies. This success was now transferring to his academic work. He willingly read and worked on his assignments with a renewed attitude of determination. He could succeed.

My one concern about the home study program was isolation from peers. Our teacher's music program included group classes and performance parties. Jeff would each month meet with other students and their families to learn about instruments, composers, music history, and more. He prepared a complex presentation for group class about aleatoric music and the composers John Cage and Charles Ives. He and his sister also led the group class in creating an impromptu aleatoric piece for the group class ensemble.

Jeff was always excited to perform at the mini-recitals. He even begged us to buy him a new coat for the events. He reveled in the applause that followed his polished performances. He especially worked on dynamics and phrasing and knew that he was a capable musician. Performing in a safe environment built his confidence and desire to try new experiences without fearing failure. He was not isolated but enjoying a music community.

Slowly the music therapist began to introduce Jeff to note reading. She began with a large print book that eliminated any visual confusion and later moved to normal size print, motivating him with his favorite seasonal songs. Learning to read music was his last hurdle in a becoming a musician but proved to be an invaluable skill in high school and college, where he participated in choirs, musicals, and instrumental groups. He became a percussionist in band and joined a local theater group to receive lead roles. We soon discovered that Jeff's strongest asset was his voice.

In his teenage years, Jeff endured another set of diagnostic tests and was diagnosed with finger agnosia, a rare neurological disorder in which the signals from the brain that instruct the fingers are interrupted. Finally, we had a reason for Jeff's limitations, not an excuse. Playing the piano had actually helped him overcome his disability and taught him how to compensate.

This struggling little boy who every educator had labeled as a hopeless failure had one of the main roles in Haydn's operetta, *La Canterina*, last year and looks forward to a bright future career. Music was the tangible key that unlocked the door to a rich and fulfilling life.

Adults

I could not trust anyone as a child. I grew up with an alcoholic father who suffered with paranoid schizophrenia. He physically, emotionally, and sexually abused me. My mother was powerless to stop him; he abused her too. My father idolized Hitler. My childhood was a nightmare. I wanted to die.

I loved to listen to the radio when I was a young child. The music filled me up and gave me hope. I longed to study the piano. Somehow I knew that I deserved a better life. My mom played the piano but was unable to teach me. She was barely surviving. It was torturous to feel the music in my body and not be able to express it. Finally, I was able to take piano lessons when I was ten years old. My dad used it as a further opportunity to punish me. He would lock me in a room to practice, telling me that I was awful and would never succeed. I learned to always expect failure.

My piano teacher was kind and suspected that something was wrong at home. She saw that I was nervous, anxious, and fearful. My teacher tried to talk to my mom but was unsuccessful. After a few months, we moved (which was a frequent pattern), and the piano lessons ended. The abuse continued, and I left home when I was fifteen years old.

I never stopped wanting to make music or play the piano. Whenever I had the chance, I listened to all types of music and socialized with musicians. I was hungry for music in my life. Now as an adult, I am finally taking the piano lessons that I longed for as a child. Music has been my lifeline and continues to bring me healing.

I have illnesses which are common in abuse victims who have suffered years of intense stress. I suffer with post-traumatic stress disorder, chronic fatigue syndrome, fibromyalgia, and arthritis. I am often in severe pain and have suffered with depression. I once medicated my pain with alcohol and drugs and am now in recovery, aware of the chemical imbalances in my body. I am easily distracted and overwhelmed, struggling to keep focused. I fight hard every day to function normally.

Experiencing music releases endorphins and fights depression, which helps ease my pain. Correct posture at the piano has helped with back pain. Studying the piano has increased my ability to concentrate.

Playing the piano and attending lessons distract me from pain, yet I often experience anxiety before coming to my lesson. I am overwhelmed with simple, everyday tasks, much less the complex task of playing an instrument. Then I start to make music at my lesson, relax, and think, "I love this. I can do this." And if I can do this, it will transfer to other areas of my life.

Music reaches me in the depths of my soul and has given me a new purpose in life. Making music has brought me physical, mental, emotional, and spiritual healing.

Note: Music is processed in the limbic system of the brain. The thalamus in the limbic area releases endorphins and other chemicals, which are natural mood elevators and pain reducers. Endorphins are more easily produced when we are in a relaxed, unstressed, state.

Note: To help them be completely honest, parents and students have requested to remain anonymous. I am grateful for their willingness to share their life stories as a way to encourage other families.

Conclusion

Celebrating Principles of an Inclusive Music Community

As we come to the end of our journey, my hope is that you have caught the vision of celebrating the joy of music making with your students. May the following ten principles of developing a music community continue to guide and encourage you:

1. The music community is interactive, and students in a cooperative setting can celebrate learning together. The family-centered approach welcomes parents and siblings.

2. Effective music education is brain compatible and joyfully engages students.

3. Students must be encouraged to see music making as relevant and useful in their daily lives.

4. Learning to make music, especially playing an instrument, is the ultimate brain compatible experience and neural networker, integrating auditory, visual, kinesthetic, affective, and cognitive neural systems in the brain.

5. The well-being of students, with their uniquely wired brains, learning styles, strengths, and needs, is more important than any single method. Teachers can synthesize different approaches to offer the best individualized program for each student. Building character and confidence in our students and cultivating compassion is more important than teaching isolated music skills.

6. The music community is inclusive, a place where all ages and abilities can make a contribution. No one is too young or too old to participate. Abilities, not disabilities, are our starting point.

7. Labels are unwelcome. Our focus is on strengths and ability development. We communicate the resiliency message to students: "What is right with you is stronger than what is wrong with you."

8. More important than being music educators, we are mentors. The one-on-one relationship, in which students feel that they are genuinely cared for and safe, is the most powerful motivator for learning. Our message is, "You will succeed. My job is to help you."

9. Experiencing the arts, specifically music making, is one of the most effective tools for overcoming adversity and avoiding destructive behavior patterns. Competence breeds confidence.

10. Our goal is to develop independent, functional, active musicians who will enjoy music making for a lifetime and will contribute to the music community in our world.

GO CELEBRATE!

Bibliography

Bitcon, Carol. *Alike and Different: The Clinical and Educational Use of Orff-Schulwerk.* Santa Ana, CA: Rosha Press, 1976.

Campbell, Don. *Introduction to the Musical Brain.* St. Louis, MO: MMB Music, 1983.

Campbell, Don. *The Mozart Effect.* New York, NY: Avon Books, 1997.

Choksy, Lois, et al. *Teaching Music in the 20th Century.* Englewood Cliffs, NJ: Prentice-Hall, 1986.

Choksy, L. *The Kodály Method.* Englewood Cliffs, NJ: Prentice-Hall, 1988.

Findlay, Elsa. *Rhythm and Movement: Applications of Dalcroze Eurhythmics.* Miami, FL: Summy Birchard, 1971.

Gardner, Howard. *Frames of Mind: The Theory of Multiple Intelligences.* New York, NY: Harper Collins, 1989.

Gardner, Howard. *Art, Mind, and Brain: A Cognitive Approach to Creativity.* New York, NY: Basic Books, 1982.

Gibbs, Jeanne. *Tribes: A New Way of Learning Together.* Santa Rosa, CA: Center Source Publications, 1994.

Green, Barry. *The Inner Game of Music.* Garden City, NY: Anchor Press, 1986.

Hart, Leslie. *How the Brain Works.* New York, NY: Basic Books, 1975.

Hart, L. *Human Brain and Human Learning.* New York, NY: Longman, 1983.

Henderon, Nan, Benard, Bonnie, & Sharp-Light, Nancy. *Resiliency In Action.* San Diego, CA: Resiliency In Action, Inc., 1999.

Honda, Masaaki. *Suzuki Changed My Life.* Miami, FL: Summy Birchard, 1984.

Jacques-Dalcroze, Emile. *Rhythm, Music, and Education.* London: Riverside Press, 1967.

Jenkins, Edward. *Primer of Braille Music.* Louiseville, KY: American Printing House for the Blind.

Bibliography

Jensen, Eric. *Arts with the Brain in Mind.* Alexandria, VA: Association for Supervision and Curriculum Development, 2001.

Johnson, D. & Johnson, R. *Cooperation and Competition: Theory and Research.* Edina, MN: Interaction Book Company, 1989.

Johnson, D., & Johnson, R. *Learning Together and Alone: Cooperative, Competitive, and Individualistic Learning.* Englewood Cliffs, NJ: Prentice-Hall, 1987.

Kaplan, Phyllis, & Stauffer, Sandra. *Cooperative Learning in Music.* Reston, VA: Music Educators National Conference, 1994

Karns, Michelle. *How to Create Positive Relationships with Students.* Champaign, IL: Research Press, 1994.

Krolick, Bettye. *How to Read Braille Music.* San Diego, CA: Opus Technologies, 1998.

Landers, Ray. *The Talent Education School of Shinichi Suzuki: An Analysis.* Smithtown, NY: Exposition, 1980.

Landis, B., & Carder, P. *The Eclectic Curriculum in Music Education: Dalcroze, Kodály, and Orff.* Reston, VA: MENC, 1972.

Levine, Mel. *A Mind At a Time.* New York, NY: Simon & Shuster, 2002.

Levine, Mel. *The Myth of Laziness.* New York, NY: Simon & Shuster, 2002.

Margulies, N. *Mapping Inner Space: Learning and Teaching Mindmapping.* Village of Oak Creek, AZ: Zephyr Press, 1991.

Mills, E., & Murphy, T. *The Suzuki Concept.* Berkeley, CA: Diablo, 1973.

Saliba, K. *Accent on Orff: An Introductory Approach.* Englewood Cliffs, NJ: Prentice-Hall, 1991.

Schonberg, Harold. *The Lives of the Great Composers.* New York, NY: W. W. Norton & Company, 1997.

Smith, Frank. *To Think.* New York, NY: Teachers College Press, 1990.

Springer, S., & Deutsch, G. *Left Brain, Right Brain.* San Francisco, CA: W. H. Freeman, 1981.

Starr, W. & C. *To Learn with Love.* Miami, FL: Summy-Birchard, 1983.

Suzuki, Shinichi. *Ability Development from Age Zero.* Miami, FL: Summy-Birchard, 1981.

Suzuki, S. *Nurtured by Love.* Miami, FL: Summy-Birchard, 1973.

Suzuki, S. *Where Love is Deep.* Athens, OH: Ability Development, 1982.

Szabo, H. *The Kodály Concept of Music Education.* New York, NY: Boosey and Hawkes, 1968.

Taylor, J., Barry, N., & Walls, K. *Music and Students at Risk: Creative Solutions for a National Dilemma.* Reston, VA: MENC, 1997.

Von Oech, R. *A Whack on the Side of the Head.* New York, NY: Warner Books, 1983.

Wilson, F., & Roehmann, F. *Music and Child Development: The Biology of Music Making.* St. Louis, MO: Magnamusic Baton, 1990.

Wycoff, J. *Mindmapping.* New York, NY: Berkeley Books, 1991.

Contact for more information:

American Association of Kodály Educators
1457 South 23rd St.
Fargo, ND 58103

American Music Therapy Association
8455 Colesville Rd., Suite 930
Silver Spring, MD 20910

American Orff Schulwerk Association
PO Box 391089
Cleveland, OH 44139

American Printing House for the Blind

1839 Frankfort Ave.

PO Box 6085

Louisville, KY 40206

Dalcroze Society of America

School of Music

Duquesne University

Pittsburg, PA 15282

Music Educators National Conference

1806 Robert Fulton Dr.

Reston, VA 20191

Music Section, National Library Service for the Blind and Physically Handicapped

Library of Congress

1291 Taylor St., NW

Washington, DC 20542

Resiliency in Action, Inc.

PO Box 90319

San Diego, CA 92169

Suzuki Association of the Americas

1900 Folsom St. #101

Boulder, CO 80302